WHAT *REALLY* MAKES

CPA FIRMS

PROFITABLE?

Second Edition

ALSO BY MARC ROSENBERG AND ROSENBERG ASSOCIATES

For more information or to order additional titles visit:
rosenbergassoc.com

Connect with Marc:
marc@rosenbergassoc.com

Connect with Kristen:
kristen@rosenbergassoc.com

WHAT *REALLY* MAKES
CPA FIRMS
PROFITABLE?

Second Edition

MARC ROSENBERG, CPA
with KRISTEN RAMPE, CPA

ROSENBERG
ASSOCIATES

CONTENTS

1

The Essence of
CPA Firm Profitability

Organizations should never have profitability as a goal. Why? Because profitability should be the *result* of an organization's efforts to manage the firm effectively, not its goal. Profitability is a *measure of success* in accomplishing core business goals. The Walt Disney Company probably said it best in a since-abandoned mission statement that was short and sweet but very powerful:

"To make millions happy."

Disney super-pleases parents by creating hundreds of lovable characters, movies and television shows that children (and a lot of adults!) adore and by creating theme parks that tap into our fantasies and imagination. They create the Disney magic by operating their entertainment facilities with a fastidious devotion to efficiency and cleanliness, a fanatical attention to the tiniest details and by countless other efforts.

Disney's customers not only pay handsomely for their access to Disney, but they do so with a smile on their faces, and they keep coming back for more. At Disney the philosophy is clear: Create and maintain a world-class organization that satisfies the customers' needs, and the profits will come as a result.

The same theme is true with CPA firm profitability. To be truly profitable, firms need to successfully achieve business goals *other than profitability*. Then, and only then, will they be profitable.

An Easy Way to Increase Profitability?

Do you want to find easy, quick ways to increase profitability? Do you want to hear about proprietary techniques that have never before been made public? Do you want to discover revolutionary ways to cut costs? Do you want to find a way to increase productivity without establishing partner accountability?

If your answer to any of these questions is yes, I'm afraid this book may disappoint you.

If your firm is not profitable today, there are no *easy* ways to turn things around. There are few quick fixes. Many of the ideas we'll present embrace concepts that you may already be familiar with. Properly applied, they work. Some work better than others, and some techniques are preferable to others, depending upon your firm's current situation. But they *do* work.

The approaches suggested in this book are based upon our experiences working with over 1,000 firms. The ideas presented are not merely *our* suggestions; they are the techniques used by the most profitable and successful firms in this country.

What Does Profitability Mean?

Let's clarify what we mean by "profitable." At CPA firms, profits are often measured with an imperfect figure called Income per (Equity) Partner, or IPP. We'll explain why it's imperfect in the next section. For now, let's agree that "profits" represent revenues less expenses and excludes any direct or indirect compensation to partners.

It's important to distinguish between *profits* and *compensation*. Many firms keep their financial statements using corporate-type accounting. They treat compensation to partners as a salary expense and show "profits" as the bottom line, which is essentially the money or profit left over after partner compensation. But in substance, it's essentially undistributed profits.

One way to analyze the profitability of a firm is to benchmark against credible national MAP surveys, such as The Rosenberg Survey. For example, let's say a firm has five partners and the total income for the five is $2 million. The IPP is $400,000. This income certainly enables the partners to enjoy a very nice living. But what if The Rosenberg Survey shows the average IPP of all firms is $500,000? Does that make the firm unprofitable? No, it does not. It merely means that the firm earns less than the industry average.

Don't Ask a CPA What Profitability Means

If you asked the president of a Fortune 500 company or the owner of a widget manufacturer to define profitability, they would be able to give a quick, definitive answer. Not so with CPAs. Surely you've heard the story, perhaps apocryphal, of the company that was interviewing for a new CPA firm. Only one question was asked of each candidate: "How much is two plus two?" The firm that won the client gave the answer "How much would you like it to be?"

The same can be true of CPA firm profitability. How do we measure it? You would think that the uncontested champions of measuring financial data, CPAs, would have this down to a science. But such is not the case.

The two most common measures are income per partner and partner income as a percentage of fees. Income as a percent of fees commonly ranges from 30–35%, with the most profitable firms earning 40% or more. But each measure has some significant flaws, all relating to the standards used for making someone a partner. Some firms have very high standards for partner promotions. (Throughout this book, the term "partner" means *equity* partner unless otherwise noted.) Others are quite generous in bestowing the partner title. Since the computation of these two measures of profitability depends on the number of partners in a firm, and the standards for who is invited to be a partner vary widely from firm to firm, it can be difficult to compare either IPP or income as a percentage of fees from firm to firm.

I've read some articles citing a number of more scientific methods for measuring profitability. A few of these articles suggest that the income statement of the typical CPA firm fails to consider the owners' labor and capital. Therefore, these expenses need to be imputed. For example, you might impute the cost of owners' labor by multiplying their billing rate times the firm's billing rate multiple. After imputing these costs, a typical firm's net income as a percent of fees might be 10-12% instead of 30-40% under the more traditional methods.

Although this approach seems inherently logical, there are serious flaws in it. Firms with high billing rates—which have consistently been shown to have among the highest correlations to financial success in CPA firms (see below)—will show higher imputed salaries for the partners and thus lower net income. This makes no sense. Also, firms that require partners to maintain significant levels of capital will have higher interest expense imputed, which results in lower net income. This too distorts the picture.

The best definition of profitability is a blend of the following:

1. **What the firm's budgeted profits are.** Some firms—not many, in my experience—actually do for themselves what they do for their clients: They estimate their expenses and revenues, and the difference between the two is the *budgeted* profit. Very simple. If the budget calls for the partners to each earn $300,000, and the firm actually earns $400,000 per partner, then they are "profitable."

2. **What the partners *want* to earn.** Everyone has different standards. I know some partners who earn $250,000 a year and don't know what to do with their money. Conversely, I know other partners who earn over $500,000 a year and seem to live paycheck to paycheck. To some, quality of life is paramount and they aren't willing to sacrifice their personal lives to make a few more bucks. To others, making more money is the driving force in their lives. They can never earn enough.

This definition may not be as satisfying as some of the more traditional measures. And I certainly am not suggesting that firms ignore the traditional measures used in MAP surveys, such as income per partner. But a blend of what your budget is with how much you want to earn is probably the best measure of firm profitability.

Now that we've defined profitability, what are the quickest and most reliable ways to get it? This will be the focus of the remainder of this book.

A Deep Dive on Partner Income as a Percentage of Fees

In my 20-plus years consulting to CPA firms, I have developed a number of pet peeves. One of them is the misguided adoration of the metric "partner income as a percentage of fees (revenue)." It's natural in all uses of statistics in all walks of life to conclude that a higher percentage is synonymous with higher profits and a lower percentage is not as good. But CPA partners should be more sophisticated in their analysis of their firm's profitability. Here's why.

Let's start with some actual data from of the 2021 Rosenberg MAP Survey:

- Firm A has income per partner (IPP) of $622,000, which translates to 23.3% of partner income as a percentage of fees.

- Firm B has IPP of $269,000 or 38.6% of partner income as a percentage of fees.

If you use IPP as the best measure of profitability, clearly Firm A is more profitable. But if you use income as percentage of fees, then Firm B is the winner.

The key data missing from the above analysis is the ratio of professional staff to partner: Firm A's ratio is 10.4 and Firm B's is 3.9. Firm A is more leveraged than Firm B and thus, spends more money on staff salaries and benefits. Because of this phenomenon, Firm A's income as a percentage of fees is lower than Firm B's. But I don't think anyone would conclude that Firm B is more profitable than Firm A.

Here are some other excerpts from The Rosenberg Survey:

Firm size	Income per partner		Income as % of fees	
	Staff-partner ratio > 8.0	Staff-partner ratio <4.0	Staff-partner ratio > 8.0	Staff-partner ratio <4.0
Over $20M	$821,000	$545,000	25%	45%
$10-$20M	$637,000	$493,000	24%	41%
$5-$10M	$779,000	$362,000	25%	35%
$2-$5M	$850,000	$340,000	29%	36%

The data clearly shows that you cannot measure the true profitability of a firm accurately by looking solely at income as a percentage of fees. What is the differentiator between IPP and income as a percentage of fees? It's leverage.

A final note: Firms with the highest leverage are more profitable today. Equally important, they are better positioned for profitability and success in the *future* because they do a better job at developing their staff. At the same time, higher-leveraged firms keep their partners away from work that can be delegated to staff so that they can focus on higher-level partner duties such as developing business, managing client relationships, managing the firm and mentoring staff.

Beware of LUBRM to Measure Profitability

I've had two mentors in my public accounting career. One I knew quite well on a personal level: Irwin Friedman, founder and MP of a huge Chicago-area CPA firm. And one I didn't know on a *personal* level, but I heard him speak often and read with awe his landmark books: consultant and Harvard business professor David Maister. Mentors are great, but they aren't perfect. I learned a lot from Maister's teachings, but he was off base on his concept of LUBRM.

LUBRM was Maister's way of defining profitability. He presented them in a formula:

- Leverage x Utilization x Billing Rate x Realization x Margin = Income per Partner

Maister didn't intend for his formula to actually be computed; he was merely stating his opinion of the five most important factors in profitability. Regrettably, this hasn't stopped some in our profession from making this calculation. It pains me to see it.

The following definitions, which interestingly are not from Maister but others *interpreting* Maister, are fairly straightforward:

- **Leverage** is the ratio of professional staff to equity partners.

- **Utilization** is measured by calculating the average annual billable hours by professional staff. This is not the proper definition of utilization, but let's not quibble.

6

- **Billing rate** is a firm's revenue divided by its overall billable hours.

- **Realization** is the percentage of firm-wide billable hours that is actually billed.

- **Margin** is the total equity partner income divided by the revenue of the firm.

Why the LUBRM Calculation Is Misguided

1. The LUBRM formula makes it appear as though each factor is evenly weighted in determining profitability. Such is not the case. Leverage and billing rate are much more significant factors in profitability than the other three.

2. Some LUBRM factors really aren't all that relevant.

    a. Realization. Hold on! I'm not saying that realization isn't important. My point is that the majority of firms experience realization percentages within a narrow band of 80-90%, so it's not a big differentiator of profitability between firms. One reason why many firms' realization is well below 90% is because they have high billing rates. A smart management technique is to set billing rates high and be willing to write off time that can't be billed due to the high rates. So it's more important to set high billing rates to increase profitability and not be so concerned about relatively "low" realization.

    b. Utilization. The argument here is similar to the one for realization. The vast majority of firms post average billable hours for their staff of between 1,450 and 1,525. So it's not as big a profit differentiator as one might think.

    c. Margin. A few pages ago, we debunked the belief that partner income as a percentage of profits is a useful way to measure CPA firm profitability.

3. LUBRUM ignores *the* two most important factors in determining firm profitability: revenue per equity partner and revenue per person. More on this in a page or two.

So the LUBRM formula doesn't work. If you come across material that uses LUBRM, ignore it.

No Recipes Available, But Here Are Some Tasty Morsels

I've often told my clients that if CPA firms did everything "right," they could easily double or triple their income. Doing things right includes several major accomplishments: bringing in lots of clients, charging strong billing rates, maintaining solid realization, leveraging a high ratio of staff to partners and keeping expenses reasonable. It's the rare firm that deserves an A in *all* of these areas.

The path to profitability is different for every firm. But the truly profitable firms achieve all of the following:

1. **Strong billing rates**. An acquaintance of mine owns a construction company. I asked him who his CPA firm was and whether or not he was satisfied with it. His response: "He's expensive, but he's good." That's how all firms should want their clients to think of them.

   On the surface, it might seem overly simplistic to suggest that raising billing rates will increase profitability. Of course it will. But the issue of billing rates runs deeper. Strong billing rates are a barometer of four important attributes of the way firms operate their business.

   a. First, billing rates are an indication of how well you convey value to your client. CPAs are quick to point out how competitive the market is. They claim that if their rates are too high, their clients will leave them for a cheaper firm. Indeed, clients often tell their former CPAs that fees were the reason for the change. But that's just an easy out for the client: studies consistently show that fees are way down on the list of what causes clients to change CPAs or become dissatisfied with their firms.

      Issues related to quality of service (lack of timeliness, tardy return of phone calls, functioning like number crunchers instead of business advisors, lack of contact, etc.) always rise to the top of the list of factors causing dissatisfaction.

   b. Second, billing rates are an indication of how well you differentiate your firm in the market. CPAs have a tendency to view themselves as one of several fine firms in their market. But there are ways to achieve noticeable differentiation: specialization, consulting services, stability, longevity, size, growth rate, activity in the community and an exemplary reputation with key referral sources such as banks and law firms are just a few techniques.

Remember: differentiated service of an undifferentiated product commands a premium.

c. Third, billing rates reflect how well you *provide value* to clients. CPAs have a strong tendency to undervalue themselves. They think that because they are doing work that the client needs but doesn't always want (compliance work), the client will not pay "high" rates. Clients may, in fact, balk at paying high rates, but this probably is a reflection of CPAs' failure to provide sufficient value to their clients rather than the clients' predisposition to be cheap.

d. Fourth, to some extent billing rates align with the level of work performed. For example, a partner who does the work of a young staff person may have a difficult time commanding a high billing rate. Partners need to leverage themselves by pushing down work instead of doing staff-level work. Higher billing rates are more easily accepted when partners do partner-level work.

2. **High staff billable hours**. I am always skeptical of MAP surveys for two reasons. First, I have found that many of these surveys contain inaccuracies regarding the way that certain metrics are computed, especially billable hours. Second, the surveys tend to perpetuate a sense that *average* is acceptable.

Here's an example. I am frequently asked by partners: "What is the national norm for billable hours for professional staff?" I might tell them 1,500. The next sound I hear is a sigh of relief from the partners, followed by the comment: "That's good to hear. Our firm is at 1,520, so we're OK."

I respond: "Congratulations, you can all feel good that your firm is a nice *average* firm."

There are several reasons why firms experience low levels of staff billable hours. Among them:

• The firm is reluctant to convey its expectations to staff for billable hour levels for fear that the staff will leave. The reality: As long as the *total* hour requirements don't go up, the staff will work 1,600 or 1,700 or more billable hours. Year after year, The Rosenberg MAP Survey shows that 25% or so of all 360 firms achieve staff billable hours in the 1600s and 1700s. It *can* be done. Contrary to some partners' perception, today's young people like to be busy.

- The firm is reluctant to be honest in conveying negative performance feedback for fear that the staff will leave. Reality: Staff crave feedback, and they won't improve without it.

- The firm has ineffective staff scheduling that, among other things, has resulted in partners losing sight of one of the fundamental duties of a partner: to keep staff busy.

- For various reasons, none of which are acceptable, partners *like* doing staff-level work. So they do it.

There is no reason why the professional staff can't average in the 1,600s or 1,700s. Many of the more profitable firms do this. Don't be content merely *meeting* MAP survey norms. Sometimes those norms are too low.

3. **High ratio of staff to (equity) partner.** This is commonly referred to as partner leverage. To the extent that a firm can achieve a high ratio of staff to partner, it will usually make more money. This is probably one of the main reasons why the large national firms make so much more money than the smaller firms. Their ratios approach 10:1, while smaller firms are in the 2.0 to 4.0 range.

   It takes several things to achieve high leverage. First, partners must be delegators instead of doers. Second, the firm must be effective at training. Third, the firm must be a good place for people to work, which keeps the staff energy level and engagement high and its turnover low. Firms with high staff turnover almost always have a catch-22 situation with the partners' attitude toward the staff: The partners get frustrated with the turnover and think it's not worth the effort to delegate and train the staff because they can do the work quicker and better—and at a higher billing rate. This situation is obviously not conducive to achieving a high ratio of staff to partners, developing the staff's knowledge and developing people as leaders.

4. **High fees per partner.** To excel at this very important measure of leverage, partners need to be good delegators and be effective at bringing in business. They also need to have a good mix of large and small clients. Partners that excel at this metric avoid administration

like the plague. Finally, the firm needs to be a great place to work for well-trained staff and have high standards for promotion to partner.

5. **High fees per person.** This metric is a measure not only of leverage but also of firm efficiency. Firms that make full use of technology, have efficient work processes, and provide good supervision and training will excel in this critically important metric.

An Elementary Economics Lesson

In any business, there are only two ways to increase profits: increase revenues or decrease expenses. CPA firms have few opportunities to decrease costs because most expenses are fixed (including most of the labor) instead of variable. Besides, CPA firms have never been known to be extravagant spenders. Therefore, it makes sense for firms to focus their attention on the top line. CPA firms are top-line-oriented businesses: Increased revenues mostly drop directly to the bottom line.

This is illustrated in the graph on the next page. Look at the cost section. As you can see, a large portion of the costs are fixed, with a smaller portion as variable. This may initially seem inaccurate because intuitively, we would classify salaries as variable. But as a practical matter, staffing levels and salaries rarely fluctuate in the short term. The number of staff maintained by a CPA firm rarely changes with small fluctuations in revenue.

One exception is when revenues continually increase at a pace that is way above average, say 15% or more. Another exception is layoffs in a recession.

As the graph shows, the fastest path to higher profits is by increasing revenues. This can be done in any number of ways: increased rates, higher levels of productivity, new clients, higher realization. The graph isn't particular to any one approach. Firms simply need to find ways to increase the slope of the revenue line. If they succeed at this, higher profits will quickly result.

11

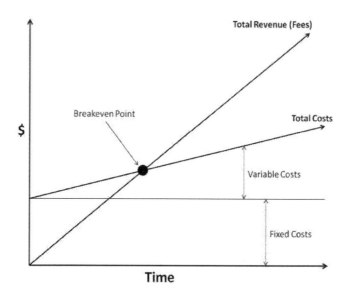

A Final Word on What Drives CPA Firm Profitability

Short and sweet, what drives profitability can be summarized this way:

As the partners go, so goes the firm.

We'll be repeating this mantra several times throughout the book. It simply means that the partners drive the firm. Partners were put on this earth to:

1. Bring in business.

2. Provide world-class service to clients that causes them to stay.

3. Grow their clients' fees.

4. Manage the firm.

5. Train, supervise and mentor staff.

The firm's staff is also critically important to profitability, but they don't begin to impact the firm's income like the partners.

The more a firm can get great performance from its partners in the five areas above, the higher its profitability will be.

2

Strong Management and Leadership: The Most Reliable Path to Profitability

If partners of firms across the country were asked to identify the key to the success of legendary Fortune 500 companies such as Apple, Google, Amazon, General Electric, Coca-Cola, IBM and countless others, I'm sure the words "strong management" and "strong leadership" would dominate their responses. Yet ask those same partners to evaluate their own firms' management, and if they were honest, their responses would not be very flattering.

Of all of the techniques for improving CPA firm profitability, none is more effective than strong management and leadership. Yet nothing is more elusive. Why is this? Perhaps it's because CPAs aren't trained to manage a firm. Perhaps they don't have time for it because their clients are deemed more important. Perhaps the firm's partners are afraid of management because inherently they know it will ultimately require them to be more accountable for their performance.

Perhaps it's the partnership form of organization (even if firms are corporations, most still operate as partnerships) that is to blame. It breeds a partner attitude of "I am an owner, so no one has the right to tell me what to do." Many CPA firms have yet to realize that their #1 client is their firm.

Good managers and leaders:

1. Identify challenges and focus people's attention on those challenges.

2. Are visionary in their thinking. Leaders constantly find new things the firm needs to do. They innovate. Coasting or complacency is not allowed.

3. Persuade people to do what they don't want to do, or what they're too lazy to do, and like it (as Harry Truman said).

4. Hold people accountable for their performance. Not by beating them up when they fall short, but by encouraging them and helping them succeed. I've read multiple times that personal accountability is doing the right thing when *no one* is looking.

5. Make decisions crisply.

Specifically, in a CPA firm, good management makes sure the firm:

1. Has a strategic plan that gets implemented.

2. Provides consulting services to broaden its service portfolio and thus, greater satisfy its clients' needs.

3. Markets proactively.

4. Has a means of holding partners accountable for their performance and behavior.

5. Tends to the basics: quality control, billing, collection, productivity, people development, etc.

6. Maintains good partner relations and communications.

7. Provides an attractive place for staff to work and stay.

Strong management, through the managing partner and others, influences everyone's behavior and gets them to accomplish these goals. *There is no greater way to improve the bottom line.*

The Proper Management Structure

The vast majority of CPA firms are well under 100 people and don't need the formalized structure that larger firms need. But virtually *all* firms, regardless of size, need *some* minimum form of structure.

There is a natural tendency for firms to minimize the role of management. There are several reasons for this:

1. The partners feel their firm is too small for formal management.

2. The partners don't really understand what management is.

3. The partners understand what management is but don't want to do it. Founders in particular are happy to shed the red tape and bureaucracy from their prior firm, not realizing that many of these practices had a good reason for being and only need to be right-sized for their new firm.

4. The partners claim they are "too busy" for management. They feel that the vast majority of their time should be spent getting clients, keeping clients and doing client work. This devotion to clients leaves virtually no time for anything else.

5. The partners feel they all must participate in all decisions, and therefore the only management they know and trust is the "management" that takes place at a partners' meeting.

Many firms have a concept of management that is the result of bad experiences at other firms. A good example is fear of the autocratic managing partner. At previous firms, some partners may have been subjected to the rule of a powerful, dominating managing partner. This person may have made decisions unilaterally, refused to seek the input of other partners or intimidated people. Partners who have lived through this type of regime are often determined never again to work under such conditions. They have seen the ugly side of what a managing partner can be and want no part of it.

The pendulum swings to the other side when firms define management as "ruling by democracy." They may designate someone as managing partner, but that person really functions as an administrative partner, preparing the firm's financial statements, hiring support personnel and procuring insurance, among many other tasks. This kind of MP may even run the partner meetings, but they are really functioning as a firm administrator rather than a managing partner. At such a firm, the managing partner has minimal authority and virtually all decisions are made by consensus at partner meetings.

The ideal structure for a CPA firm is outlined below. These positions generally apply more to larger than smaller firms.

Managing Partner Role

Here's why firms need a managing partner:

1. **Someone needs to be the visionary for the firm.** Someone needs to be thinking of what the firm should look like in the future. That future could be six months out, a year out, two years ahead or five. Equally important is a tenacious focus on *implementing* the vision. The managing partner needs to be the one person in the firm who makes sure the firm looks ahead for ideas. Good managing partners are *never* content with the status quo.

2. **A managing partner provides focus to the firm.** Perhaps the best explanation for why management is so difficult for firms is the difficulty of balancing client-related duties with internal duties and responsibilities. When a partner must choose between client and internal needs, the client will always come first. But this choice can take its toll on the firm. Never having time for non-client activities such as marketing, developing new services and nurturing staff can be just as harmful to a firm's long-term success as neglecting clients or losing revenue. Managing partners must help their firm decide what the "first things" are, and then *put* them first, day by day.

3. **Decisions need to be made promptly.** One of the biggest flaws of the "management by committee" style is that committees are inherently slow or reluctant to make decisions. Attempts at compromise often result in watered-down decisions, or no decisions at all. It's difficult for eight partners as a group, sitting around a table, to make bold, intelligent, swift decisions on the firm's issues.

4. **Someone needs to hold partners accountable for their performance and behavior.** As the partners go, so goes the firm. Partners who are accountable for their performance and behavior perform better than those who are not. Equally important, firms that achieve

partner accountability are more *profitable* than firms that don't. It's critically important that the firm has systems in place to hold partners accountable. More importantly, the firm needs a strong managing partner who holds partners accountable.

Some firms have "true" managing partners while others really have MPs who function more like administrative partners. There are three main things that distinguish the two:

- A true MP manages and supervises the other partners.

- A true MP holds partners accountable; an administrative partner does not.

- A true MP is responsible for driving the firm's revenue growth and profitability.

5. **Someone must be tirelessly devoted to making the firm a great place to work,** for staff especially but also for partners. The firm must walk the talk when it proclaims that its staff are just as important as its clients.

Most would agree that the performance of the staff is critically important to the firm's overall success and profitability. So it logically follows that one of the most important jobs of the MP is to personally drive this initiative. The MP must be driven to achieving the goal of having a great staff that is engaged, well-trained and upwardly mobile. Certainly, the vast majority of the work on this goal will be done by the partners and other leaders, but the firm needs an MP who will lead the charge.

Other Essential Roles

Firm Administrator or COO. Management and administration are both important. But management operates at a much higher level and more strategically than administration. Also, firm administrators cost a lot less than managing partners. Why ask someone who earns $500,000 or more, is adept at rainmaking and commands a high billing rate to do the work of someone who typically earns $70,000-$175,000 per year, depending on firm size? It makes no sense. Firm administrators do two things for a firm: First, their presence frees up partners to do partner-level work, thus making the firm more profitable. Second, firm administrators are experienced and trained to do administration and thus are

17

more proficient at it than partners (though the partners may be reluctant to admit this!).

Executive Committee. Like all organizations of a significant size, CPA firms benefit from a board that provides advice and counsel to the managing partner. It also provides the firm with a formal mechanism for assisting MPs in carrying out their duties and performing special, high-level projects. Allocating partner income and evaluating the MP are important duties of an Executive Committee.

Once firms have at least seven partners, they should begin considering creating an executive committee. Firms with nine partners or more should definitely have an EC.

Marketing Director/Coordinator. If a firm is really serious about marketing and business development, it understands that there is a long list of support tasks in the marketing area. This list includes overseeing the firm's newsletter program, making sure the firm has brochures and other appropriate marketing materials, planning seminars, arranging speaking engagements, getting articles published, maintaining the firm's database, executing direct mail campaigns and countless other duties.

As with a firm administrator, it makes sense to hire someone to perform these tasks so that the partners can concentrate on the part of marketing that really needs their involvement: meeting face to face with prospects and clients.

Human Resources. Since the dawn of time, it has been common for firms of all sizes to designate one of their partners as the HR partner. At most firms, this position performed by a partner was nowhere near a full-time position. The focus in the past was more on the administrative aspects of HR than on seeing the big picture and helping the firm create a great environment for the staff.

Here are the differences between the administrative and higher-level approaches to human resources.

The administrative aspect of HR includes these tasks.

- Keeping personnel records.
- Screening recruits.
- Maintaining benefit policies.

- Coordinating staff appraisals.
- Communicating personnel policies throughout the firm.
- Supervising low level HR people.

The higher-level focus of HR is to make the firm a great place to work and improve staff relations.

- Increasing staff retention.
- Driving the firm's training and leadership development programs.
- Coordinating the firm's mentoring program.
- Spearheading the firm's efforts to compensate staff competitively.
- Creating job descriptions.
- Administering staff surveys.
- Being a safe place that staff can come to with problems.

An HR director is a high-level, well-paid professional who reports directly to the managing partner or to a high-level COO.

Firms are increasingly finding that the HR director needs to focus on making sure the firm treat its staff as if they're as important as clients and doing everything possible to assure that the staff is great, talented, engaged and upwardly mobile. The administrative efforts are merely the ante to get into the game.

A good HR director today must be a people person who enjoys interacting with staff, is compassionate and sensitive and has a positive attitude dealing with staff. This person doesn't have to be a partner. A manager or director who is credible to both the staff and the partners can do a great job.

The Value of Strategic Thinking

Roberto Goizueta, the late chairman of Coca-Cola and certainly one of the top two or three CEOs of the late 20th century, said it best:

> "Challenging the status quo when you have been successful is difficult. If you think you will be successful running your business in the

next 10 years the way you did the last 10 years, you're out of your mind. To succeed, we have to disturb the present."

Compared to most vocations, CPA partners make a pretty good living. Their success has been attributable primarily to a combination of the following:

1. Bringing in business.
2. Providing great service to clients, which results in client retention and moving clients upscale in terms of services.
3. Possessing strong technical skills.
4. Developing staff into leaders.
5. Having strong interpersonal skills.

Other skills are also important, such as:

- Providing consulting services.
- Niche marketing and specialization.
- Proficiency and comfort with technology.
- Getting work done by a generation of young people who have values that are quite different from, and in some cases repulsive to, older partners.
- Dealing with shortages of qualified staff.
- Providing one-stop shopping for the wide array of financial services that clients want.
- Holding personnel accountable for their performance, just like real businesses.

There will always be firms that continue to be successful by doing things as they have always done them. But those firms are the rare exceptions. Most firms realize that they must react to the above challenges, but they haven't figured out *how* to react.

Strategic thinking is critical to the future success of CPA firms. Indeed, strategic thinking and visioning is critical to the future success of *any* organization. The following evidence supports these statements:

- In their book *Built to Last,* James Collins and Jerry Porras found that visionary companies outperformed a control group by more than six to one.

- In a study of strategic planning by law firms, those firms engaging in strategic planning significantly outperformed those that didn't.

- In my personal experience with firms, I have found that the more successful firms engage in strategic planning.

The value of brainstorming the future of your firm is incalculable. It's critically important to create a picture of how you would like your firm to look in 5 to 10 years, develop *specific,* measurable goals to achieve the vision, assign the goals and deadlines to individuals, establish accountability for accomplishing the goals and implement these plans.

Many firms that I work with are stuck in the mud in the strategic planning area. They have had success doing things the same way for many years. Intuitively, they know they should make some changes to keep up with what progressive firms are doing. But they don't know how to get started. They are so busy with the present that they have no time or energy to look at the future. Others still think that the old ways will continue to work throughout their lifetime, despite what the experts say. Some leaders are afraid that the changes they will have to make are so drastic that they will no longer enjoy being CPAs.

There is a great phrase for what these firms need to do: achieve a paradigm shift. Many years ago, author Joel Barker, a pioneer in using the term "paradigm shifts," illuminated all of us with his legendary books on paradigms. He defined paradigms as "sets of rules that govern our actions. They establish boundaries. It's not important that the paradigms *are* valid. The most significant thing is that we *believe* the paradigms to be valid. Most paradigms are self-imposed and are subconscious."

Firms that are stuck in the mud have what Barker terms "paradigm paralysis" and need to achieve a paradigm shift. That's the hard part. The easy part will be counting the money when it starts coming in after they implement strategic initiatives.

The Importance of Culture

In my 20+ years of consulting to CPA firms, I have met hundreds of managing partners. Some are great MPs, regardless of their firms' size. Many have led very large, hugely successful firms that survived their founders. I have a favorite question to ask these MPs: "What accounts for your exceptional track record of growth, profitability and success?"

The hands-down winner is culture. Not rainmakers. Not great staff. Not large clients. Not technology. Not specialization. Not vision.

Culture.

Often this doesn't feel like a satisfactory answer. It seems too touchy-feely. We're all familiar with Supreme Court Justice Potter Stewart's famous definition of pornography: "It's hard to define but you know it when you see it." This definition certainly applies to culture.

Some common definitions of culture:

- The shared values, attributes, and characteristics of an organization.

- Firm members' commitment at the highest level to an engaging culture, which leads the firm to perform at an elite level.

- Getting everyone rowing in the same direction (an expression epitomized in the great book *The Boys in The Boat* by Daniel James Brown, a true story about a university team with little training at crewing that defeated the world's elite college teams, shocking the world).

- The sum total of the ways of living that are built up by the firm and transmitted from one generation to the next.

- Violations to it would be a sin if the firm were an organized religion. Firms with a strong culture never allow transgressions to the firm's most important values, policies and practices.

Sometimes I'm *still* not sure what culture really is. I find it helpful to drill down and cite things in a firm that typify a great culture:

- Both partners and staff do some things that are fun.
- The firm has strong communication and transparency; people know what's going on.
- People work as a team, not individuals.
- The partners are great bosses.
- There is accountability, especially at the partner level.
- The firm offers work-life balance and a feeling of family.
- Partners and staff adhere to the firm's vision, policies and practices.

A firm's culture is defined by the partners. If the partners don't live and breathe the firm's culture and core values, then they shouldn't expect the staff to.

Few firms under $15M have a strong culture that meets these definitions. Indeed, many smaller firms have a *negative* culture, though obviously, that's not what they aspire to. Examples include operating the firm like a sweatshop, abusive treatment by the partners or clients that leads to high turnover, a lack of effort to bring in business, no accountability and no career-pathing and mentoring for staff.

The main reason why firms don't have strong cultures is that transgressions of policies, practices and core values by the partners are tolerated. When partners see unpunished transgressions by one partner, they *all* tend to do whatever they want. When staff see the partners refusing to embrace a culture that the firm is trying to build, *they* tend to be transgressors as well.

Part of great firm management is establishing a strong culture: getting everyone buying into what the firm is all about so that everyone is rowing in the same direction.

The 25 Best Practices that Transform Good Firms into Great Firms

The 25 best practices here evolved from our observations from working with great firms for over *20 years*. We update this list often, so it varies a bit from similar lists in our other books. Few firms do them all well, but the best firms do well on most of them. The following practices are not necessarily listed in order of importance.

	Grade
1. Time management, especially effective use of nonbillable time. Time is our biggest asset; we must spend it wisely. Focus on doing first things first. Beware the obstacles: affluence, complacency and lack of accountability.	
2. Effective management structure & leadership. Hire admin professionals to keep partners out of the weeds.	
3. Strong culture: hard to define but you know it when you see it. Common focus. If the firm were an organized religion, what would be a sin?	
4. Proactive business-getting efforts; a pervasive culture of "you can't not try."	
5. Exploit potential with existing clients; increase your firm's touch points.	
6. The power of specialization and niche marketing.	
7. World-class service. Deliver technically flawless work.	
8. Be a higher-priced, lower-volume shop rather than a lower-priced, higher-volume shop.	
9. Franchised processes and procedures.	
10. Selling and servicing as a team because clients are *firm*-centric, not *partner*-centric.	
11. Maximize staff-to-partner leverage; partners are delegators, not doers.	
12. Clear strategic plan. Vision. Direction. Heavy focus on implementation. Goal setting.	
13. Right people *on* the bus & wrong people *off* the bus; common focus & culture.	

	Grade
14. Diversity of services to satisfy increasing client needs.	
15. Tenacious commitment to making your firm a great place to work. Robust recruiting. Performance feedback that helps staff learn and grow. Transparency.	
16. Proactive leadership development and mentoring. Partners are good bosses.	
17. World-class training in both technical and soft skills.	
18. Remote work: systems in place for people to work effectively from a distance; solve challenges of business development, staff mentoring, firm management and partner relations remotely. Flexibility in when and where to work.	
19. Address the challenges of increasing consulting services as compliance work declines.	
20. Succession planning; plans in place to move the firm to the next generation.	
21. Good partner relations; conflicts addressed. Transgressions from the firm's core values are not allowed.	
22. Partner accountability & good corporate citizenship: "If you're a jerk, you're out."	
23. Performance-based compensation; partner comp is aligned with what the firm needs the partners to do and where the firm needs to go. System should recognize and reward partner production as well as intangibles.	
24. Put technology to work for you. Embrace cybersecurity.	
25. Benchmarking, both for MAP statistics and for client satisfaction & loyalty.	

In the next pages, let's drill down on these 25 best practices.

1. **Time management.** At the end of each day, week, month or year, we need to optimize our most scarce resource—our time. For busy, high-level, multitasking partners of dynamic CPA firms, there will always be more things they need to do than the time to do them. So it's critical that partners individually, as well as their firms, have systems and behaviors in place to ensure that they are consistently doing the first things first.

2. **Effective management.** There is nothing more important to the growth, profitability and success of a CPA firm than effective management and leadership. It makes everything else—revenue growth, profitability, people development, succession planning— happen. Management of the firm should never take a back seat to clients. The firm should be the #1 client.

3. **Culture.** When highly successful (usually larger) firms are asked the key to their phenomenal success, the most common response is their firm's culture. Partners are on the same page. All personnel are engaged and adhere to the firm's core values and practices. They do the right things when no one is watching. So much more can be achieved when a firm has a strong culture and works as a team than when the partners are Lone Rangers with the attitude "I'm a partner and that gives me the right to do whatever I want whenever I please."

4. **Proactive business development.** Easily the most difficult important CPA firm performance attribute is bringing in business. If firms don't grow, they die, or at least they stagnate. Partners must have the mindset of sole practitioners: If they don't bring in business, nobody else will. This doesn't mean that every partner needs to be a rainmaker, but the vast majority of the firm's partners should be making an effort.

5. **Exploit the potential with existing clients.** Since many partners find it challenging to bring in business, partners need to devise strategies, plans and tactics to overcome the inherent difficulty of business development. Perhaps the most powerful of these tactics is tapping into the potential of existing clients. This means both expanded services and referrals to new clients. It's a lot easier to increase revenue from *existing* clients than to go on the street and identify and close *new* clients who don't know you.

6. **Specialization and niche marketing.** This is another tactic that makes business development easier. Many CPAs are generalists and try to be all things to all people. That's the hard way to do BD. The easier way is to develop specialties because they're easier to sell. Clients love hiring people perceived as experts, and they'll pay premium prices for the expertise. The specialty can be in a target industry such as real estate or medical practices, or it can be a service such as business valuations, technology, internal controls, international tax, forensic accounting or M&A. This doesn't mean you give up your generalist client base. You just target your BD efforts in your

specialty areas. By becoming a well-known specialist, you get to practice the CPA's favorite form of selling, simply answering the phone and saying, "Yes, I'll take your order."

7. **World-class service.** The #1 reason why clients switch CPA firms is service. It's not price. It's not even the quality of your work because clients are usually not equipped to evaluate it. Great service means being proactive. Call your clients instead of waiting for them to call you. Deliver products *before* they are expected. Introduce clients to other professionals who can help them.

8. **Be a higher-priced, lower-volume shop rather than a lower-priced, higher-volume one.** CPAs provide services that few, if any, other professionals can provide. If these services are provided with great service, clients are willing to pay a nice price for it. You want your clients to describe you like this: "My CPA is expensive but good!" A much shorter path to profitability is to be a high-priced firm. A by-product of this approach is that the firm makes more money doing less work.

    At the same time, we must recognize that we live in a world where it's hard to find staff. We live in an era of labor shortages. So we need to stop, or at least slow down, accepting any client with a heartbeat. It makes sense to reduce the number of clients served so we are less desperate to find staff. I often ask my clients: "If you raised your prices 20% (not immediately, but over a period of time), would you lose 20% of your business?" Almost everyone says no. Yet they are reluctant to raise prices.

    A final observation: Because most CPAs dislike business develop-ment, they either consciously or unconsciously set their billing rates and fees low as a marketing tactic. They reason that if they are cheap, clients will hire them. This mindset is deeply flawed.

9. **Franchised processes and procedures.** Most CPA firm partner groups are fiercely independent. They reason that being an owner of a business gives them the inalienable right to do whatever they want whenever they please. One of the most damning manifestations of this is that every partner has a different way of doing the same work procedure. This not only drives the staff crazy but results in a tre-mendous amount of inefficiency. The better firms standardize as many of their work procedures as possible so that they can operate efficiently and profitably.

10. **Clients are *firm*-centric instead of *partner*-centric.** Firms under $15M have a tendency to operate as sole practitioners practicing under one roof, sharing a common name, staff and overhead. In other words, *not* acting as a team. Even though the partners might say their clients are the *firm's* clients, in practice, they act like they are *their* individual clients. The result is that clients are underserved and are at greater risk of leaving if a partner should suddenly leave the firm. But when clients are served by a team, the expertise of multiple partners and staff is brought together to better serve clients. Cross-selling becomes natural. When clients have *multiple touch points* at the firm, they are less likely to leave if the lead partner departs the firm. *We* always trumps *I.*

11. **Maximum staff-to-partner leverage.** One of the strongest correlations to profitability is staff-to-partner leverage. When this ratio is high, partners are pushing down work to the staff, thus freeing up their time to do partner-level duties such as developing business, managing the firm and helping staff learn and grow. But when this ratio is low, it almost always means that the partners are doing staff-level work. This creates two problems:

    • Profitability is held back because the partners aren't leveraging their time. Leverage is strongly correlated to profitability.

    • Because partners are doing work that staff should be doing, they are slowing the firm's efforts to develop the staff's skills and denying them the valuable experiences of serving clients.

12. **Clear strategic plan, vision, direction.** Firms have a tendency to operate in the here and now. Partners are super-busy with their client duties, so firm-wide goals seldom get accomplished. The focus is on earning money *today* without much regard for what the firm will look like *tomorrow.* When people or organizations formalize strategy and put goals in writing, they are much more likely to achieve their goals than if the goals are merely *in their mind.*

13. **Get the right people *on* the bus and get the wrong people *off* the bus.** This Jim Collins quote is directed at firms who have negative people on board, especially in the partner ranks. They're always saying, "That will never work" or "We've tried that before and it failed." These naysayers zap everyone's energy and attitude, making it difficult for the firm to rally the troops on the firm's strategy and vision. This cancer needs to be removed before it spreads throughout the

firm. These people need to leave the firm or at least be isolated to minimize the damage before grand plans can be implemented.

14. **Diversity of services.** This one is very simple. The more services the firm offers, the more revenue it can realize because clients can be cross-sold. And the more services a firm offers, the better job it will do satisfying clients' increasingly sophisticated and diverse needs, thus increasing its ability to retain clients and grow with them.

15. **Tenacious commitment to making the firm a great place to work.** Most firms *say* that their staff are just as important as their clients. Unfortunately, many firms don't walk the talk. From recruiting to training to mentoring to providing a career path to assigning challenging work to providing exciting salaries and benefits, partners should be dead serious about making their firms great places for their staff to work.

16. **Proactive leadership development and mentoring.** The #1 factor in retaining employees *in any organization* is a person's relationship with the boss. At CPA firms, since staff work on multiple clients, they have multiple bosses, mostly partners and managers. This relationship isn't limited to the bosses being nice to work with. More importantly, it's about the bosses' effectiveness in helping their staff learn and grow and advance in the firm.

17. **World-class training.** Over the years, we have convened many staff focus groups and conducted surveys to learn how staff feel about various aspects of their jobs and the firm. One question we always ask is: "What do you think about the firm's training?" A frequent response has been "What training?" What a shame. CPA firms are by nature leveraged businesses. Depending on the firm's size, for every partner there are three to ten staff. Thus, CPA firms rely heavily on their staff. It's unfortunate when they don't train those staffers properly. Firms also have a tendency to focus exclusively on technical training and ignore training in soft skills. That's a big mistake.

18. **Remote work systems.** One result of the Covid pandemic is that remote work is here to stay—not necessarily 100% remote, but at least double what it was historically. Firms need to master skills that in the past were done face to face and now are done remotely or in a hybrid work environment. These skills include business development, training and mentoring staff, and maintaining effective relationships with clients, staff and partners.

19. **Managing the changing landscape of services offered by CPA firms,** adding consulting services as compliance work declines. Roughly 85-90% of services offered by CPA firms haven't changed for a hundred years: compliance services like audits, accounting and tax. The 10-15% of revenue that CPA firms report on MAP surveys as "consulting" are heavily tied to the compliance services like "handholding," recruiting, financial planning, etc. Bottom line: Many CPA firms fail to provide enough true consulting: business valuations, technology consulting, M&A, wealth management, risk management, strategy and many more. Predictions are that continuing technology advances will greatly reduce the revenue potential for traditional compliance services. To offset this loss, firms need to provide more consulting services. This practice is probably the most strategic challenge that CPA firms face.

20. **Succession planning.** A good 70-80% of all first-generation CPA firms never make it to the second. Why? They suck at succession planning. If done right, succession planning isn't an event triggered by partners retiring. The best way to avoid a problem—like succession planning challenges—is to never let the problem occur in the first place. Effective succession planning is a *process* that advances every time the firm brings in a new client. It requires a continuous commitment to developing leadership and making the firm a great place to work.

21. **Good partner relations.** Is there anything more conducive to working effectively than waking up in the morning, looking at yourself in the mirror and feeling excited about going to work and working with people you enjoy being with? When the partners of a firm work reasonably well together, good things happen. But when partners don't get along or don't communicate with each other, this damages teamwork, staff morale, accountability, client service and innovation. I said earlier, "As the partners go, so goes the firm." When a firm has good partner relations, it can achieve great things. But when partner relations are in the sewer, this obstacle to success is almost impossible to overcome.

22. **Partner accountability.** If there are no consequences to failing to achieve a goal or expectation (including performing one's duties), then it is less likely the goals will be accomplished or the expectations met. Accountability ensures that partners meet their goals and performance expectations. Again, "As the partners go, so goes the

firm." If partners are not held accountable for their performance and behavior, then their performance, and that of the firm, will almost assuredly suffer.

23. **Performance-based partner compensation.** Partners' compensation should have a direct link to their performance. Performance is measured in several different ways: traditional production (finder, minder, grinder), intangibles (firm management, mentoring staff and teamwork), achievement of goals and meeting expectations of one's job (department head, team leader, quality control guru). You get what you reward.

24. **Put technology to work for you.** Do I need to spell this out? Technology is easily the most significant force to impact the CPA profession in the past 50 years, and it continues to take quantum leaps forward. We've all known for years that the pace of technological change increases exponentially. Predictions for the impact of technology are truly mind-boggling. Firms need to make sure they are using technology to the fullest in order to achieve peak efficiency and profitability.

25. **Benchmarking.** Recently I began working with a small firm on an upward merger. I reviewed the firm's data and found that their full-time staff averaged 1,100 billable hours a year. When I asked the owners about this, they had no idea that productivity was low. They were stunned to hear me say that most firms' staff average about 1,500 billable hours. This firm had been living in a cocoon; they had no idea what the outside world was like. Firms need benchmarking to gauge how well they are managing their firm and identify weaknesses. Comparisons of a firm's actual performance to relevant benchmarks improve performance and thus profitability.

Warning: Remember that benchmarks are often *averages* of many firms' data. Firms need to ask themselves if they will be content merely *meeting* the averages. If they don't exceed those averages, they need to understand that they are *average* firms.

3

How Benchmarking Boosts Profits

The integrity of CPAs is consistently rated among the highest of all professionals. Primary reasons for this are dedication to client service, delivery of high-quality work and a high degree of technical excellence acquired from working with hundreds, if not thousands, of clients. Partners at many CPA firms pursue this dedication to the point of neglecting the management and profitability of their own practice. As the saying goes: "The shoemaker's children go barefoot." Benchmarking helps firms improve profitability as they continue to serve their clients.

CPA Partners often Operate in a Cocoon

"Do you feel your firm's billing rates are high, low or just where they should be?" This is an interview question I often pose to partners. A common response is "high." I then show them a survey of billing rates for comparable firms in their markets. To their surprise, they see that their rates are *below* those of their competitors. More often than not, the firm takes my hint and raises its rates, and the increased revenues fall directly to the bottom line. And few, if any, clients leave. All while the partners continue to perform their work with the same high degree of dedication, commitment and quality as before the rate increase.

This scenario illustrates the power of benchmarking. Firms should always strive to be the best they can be. But how can they do this if they don't know what "best" *is* or even what average is? That's why we need to benchmark.

Benefits of Benchmarking in a Nutshell

By comparing various statistics, ratios and metrics of your firm to other firms, preferably firms similar to yours in terms of size and geographic location, you can measure your firm's performance.

By identifying areas where performance is strong, firms are able to focus *even more* on those strengths and exploit their total potential. Too often, firms tend to focus on their metrics that are below industry norms, ignoring opportunities to build on their strengths. Examples of going beyond average:

- Billing rates are 5% above the norm. Nice, but 5% isn't a lot. Perhaps the firm feels its expertise and reputation warrant being 10% or 15% above the norm, so it increases rates.

- Staff compensation is equal to the industry norm. Perhaps in this age of labor shortages, the firm may decide to pay *more than* the competition to better attract and retain staff.

By identifying areas that warrant improvement, firms decide where to take corrective action and eliminate weaknesses. Examples of weaknesses include low billing rates, low realization and low billable hours from staff. Partners being too billable keeps staff billable hours below the industry norm.

Benchmarking Is a Three-Step Process

1. *Measuring* your firm's performance by computing various performance statistics.

2. *Analyzing* performance by comparing those statistics to other firms and industry norms.

3. *Changing* your firm's performance by exploiting strengths and curbing weaknesses.

Without benchmarking, firms inevitably lead a provincial existence, blissfully unaware of reality.

Numbers Don't Lie

We've all heard this saying. If your firm's profits are below average, benchmarking will *quickly* identify what's holding you back. I'm not suggesting for a moment that "numbers" or benchmarks are the end-all to higher profits. Factors such as management, leadership, talent, accountability and people skills are also critically important. But benchmarking is a good weapon to have in your arsenal.

10 Key Metrics Benchmarks for CPA Firms

The data in the chart below is from The 2021 Rosenberg Survey, the country's largest and most authoritative survey of CPA firm statistics serving mid-size firms.

		Annual net revenue			
Rank	Metric	Over $20M	$10-$20M	$5-$10M	$2-$5M
	Income per partner	**$688,000**	**$519,000**	**$504,000**	**$343,000**
1	Fees per ptr	$2,438,000	$1,906,000	$1,645,000	$1,102,000
2	Fees/person	$207,000	$192,000	$188,000	$179,000
3	Staff-ptr ratio	9.0	7.3	6.5	4.3
4	Ptr bill rate	$405	$355	$334	$302
5	Utilization	52%	53%	55%	55%
6	Staff bill hrs	1,499	1,477	1,508	1,450
7	Realization	86%	85%	87%	89%
8	Ptr bill hours	1,052	1,065	1,163	1,180
9	Total ptr hrs	2,415	2,436	2,482	2,368
10	% admin staff	17%	17%	18%	17%

Chart explanation: Each year, we research these ten metrics in the Rosenberg Survey Test Laboratory to see which has the strongest correlation to profitability, as measured by income per partner. The left-hand column, "Rank" indicates that correlation. The top four metrics have the strongest correlation to profitability *by far.* These top four metrics have been the same for over 20 years of our survey.

The quickest path to profitability:

- Keep the bar high for equity partner.

- Partners should be highly leveraged, managing large client bases by delegating work to staff, training the staff to do the work and mentoring them to advance in the firm.

- Strive for a high staff-partner ratio.

- Set strong billing rates. We list only partner billing rates in the chart because partner billing rates are usually a good indicator of where the rates are for staff.

I worked with a great managing partner for many years who shared with me a powerful message: "The way to make money in this business is rates and leverage. Rates and leverage."

If you are looking for a takeaway from this chapter, benchmark your firm's metrics against these ten metrics.

Compare to the Right Benchmarks

The two key ways to ensure using the correct benchmarks:

1. Compare your firm to comparably *sized* firms. If you are a $7M firm, you should be comparing yourself to $5-$10M firms, not $25M firms. The two firms' sizes are managed quite differently from one another.

2. Compare your firm to firms of comparable *market size,* as defined by the metropolitan population. If your firm is in Decatur, Illinois, you should be comparing yourself to firms in similar-sized cities, not firms in Chicago, Dallas or Phoenix.

Be skeptical of surveys that average numbers from firms of a wide range of sizes and population markets.

A Word about Averages

Several years ago, during a retreat I was facilitating for a CPA firm, the partners asked me what the national average was for staff billable hours. I responded with 1,500. One of the partners looked at another and said: "Great, we're at 1,510." Once again, we have a "nice ... *average* firm."

The moral of the story? Don't be content hitting averages. If your firm is way below the average, then the average may very well be a good target to shoot for, at least for now. But if you're close to average, you should strive to be *above* average. In this example, I'll bet many firms would be unhappy with their staff working only 1,500 billable hours out of the 2,250 hours they work for the year. Why this national norm is *only* 1,500 is a story for another day.

The 10 Biggest Mistakes in Benchmarking

I never cease to be amazed at the lack of understanding that CPA firm partners, including many managing partners, have about reading a MAP (Management of an Accounting Practice) Survey and computing MAP statistics. These difficulties prevent partners from using a MAP Survey properly for the purpose for which it was intended: to improve firm performance.

Here's a list—in no particular order—of the 10 biggest mistakes partners make in reading and computing MAP statistics. Avoid these common pitfalls and your benchmarking results will be more reliable and accurate.

1. **Overrelying on partner income percentage as a measure of profitability**. We addressed this in Chapter 1, but it bears repeating.

   Many partners have a rule of thumb (I hate rules of thumb because they often cause misinformation and faulty conclusions) that 33% is a respectable, desirable partner income percentage and that to be "truly profitable," this metric must be 40% or more.

   What firms need to understand is that this metric is impacted as much by the firm's staff-partner ratio as by innate profitability. Therefore, we caution firms to avoid making rash judgments about profitability based solely on partner income percentage.

If a firm is heavily leveraged, partner income percentages may be in the 20s and low 30s. This doesn't necessarily mean that the firm's profitability is low. It's just that when a firm is highly leveraged, which almost always correlates to high profitability, the way the math works is that the profitability *percentage* will be lower.

Conversely, if a firm is poorly leveraged, the firm's profit percentage will be higher. But it doesn't mean that the firm is highly profitable.

2. **Being content with "average."** Remember, when a MAP survey cites an average for a group of firms, it's just that—an average. To illustrate this point, let's examine data from the 2021 Rosenberg Survey:

- The national average for staff billable hours is about 1,500.

- 67 of 288 (23%) multipartner firms posted staff billable hours 1,600 or higher.

- 87 of the 288 (30%) firms got less than 1,400 billable hours from their staff.

The folly of being content with average performance is that 23% of the surveyed firms were able to achieve higher productivity from their staff. If 23% of all firms can do it, why can't yours?

3. **Averaging salary data**. I've seen many MAP surveys tabulate the average salary for various positions at firms throughout the country. Examples: A two-year tax person, a four-year audit person, a firm administrator. This is one of the most senseless pieces of information I've ever seen, yet surveys love to report it. The problem is that personnel from firms in New York City are mixed in with personnel from Montrose, Colorado and Decatur, Illinois. Personnel from a $30M firm are combined with personnel from a $3M firm. The resulting averages are utterly meaningless. Compensation data is relevant only if it is taken from a market that is comparable to your own, which is something that most MAP surveys cannot possibly do. If your firm is in Memphis, only surveys of Memphis firms will produce valid results that you can use to set compensation levels for personnel at your firm.

4. **Computing the average charge hours for any category of personnel, such as partners and professional staff.** Most firms make the mistake of computing the number of full-time employees (FTEs)

by adding up their total work hours and dividing by 2,080. This causes firms to count people with more than 2,080 hours as more than one FTE, which should never happen. This practice understates the average.

The only proper way to compute average annual charge hours for a personnel group is to include only personnel who were with the firm for a *full year* AND were *full time* the entire year. In computing the average, omit part-time personnel and personnel who began working at the firm after the year began or who left the firm before the year ended. Average annual charge hours cannot be annualized because of the skewing effect of the tax season.

If you do the math, making the incorrect computations above can distort this true metric by as much as 20-25%.

5. **Treating non-equity partners like "partners."** The problem here is in the definition. Many non-equity partners at the Top 100 firms outperform and outearn equity partners at much smaller firms. But most non-equity partners at firms below the Top 100 function (which comprises 95% or more of all multipartner firms) perform more like managers than equity partners.

Treating non-equity partners the same as equity partners for such metrics as fees per partner and ratio of staff to partner will usually distort these ratios. So it is critical to treat non-equity partners as professional staff for purposes of computing "partner" ratios.

6. **Computing income per partner.** As accountants, we certainly understand the difference between the accrual and cash basis methods of accounting. But firms often ignore this distinction when computing income per partner (IPP), and that plays havoc with the results.

There are two ways that firms commonly compute IPP for MAP Surveys. The first method starts with the firm's accrual basis net income, before any compensation to partners, and divides that by the number of partners in the firm.

The second method takes the actual *cash* paid to each partner, adds it up and computes IPP. I'm sure I don't have to tell you that the first method is correct and the second method is incorrect. The problem with using the second method stems from two factors: First, firms often decide to retain some of their income for internal operations, capital expenditures and cushion; these amounts need to be included in IPP. Second, the fluctuation from year to year in A/R and WIP produces cash earnings for the firm that differ, sometimes substantially, from net income in the income statement.

7. **Relying on utilization percentage**. This metric is the total billable hours of a firm divided by the total work hours of the firm, with all personnel included. Firms also track utilization percentage for departments, partners, managers, seniors, etc. I've never been a big fan of utilization percentage because it is easily manipulated by the total hours a person works and the extent to which people record all of their billable time. I'm more interested in knowing how realized, billable hours and dollars per person or by department compare to budget than I am in knowing the *percentage* of billable to total hours. You can't take a percentage to the bank, but you can take *dollars.*

8. **Misusing net firm billing rate**. This is calculated by taking the total annual net fees of the firm and dividing it by the total firm-wide billable hours. This rate is dramatically impacted by the firm's ratio of staff to partners.

   Here's a great example. A client of mine with long-standing profitability problems called me after reading our latest MAP survey. He lamented that, as usual, his firm lagged in almost every industry norm. But with great pride, he told me that his firm's net firm billing rate was 20% higher than the industry norm. I had to puncture his balloon by telling him: "Yes, you did well in this category, but only because you have 10 partners and 9 staff!"

   Net firm billing rates in MAP surveys are relevant only if your firm has a reasonably normal staff-partner ratio.

9. **Computing average compensation for firm administrators.** The problem here is the definition of the position "firm administrator." Some firm administrators function at a partner level and are very handsomely paid. Other firm administrators, though hard-working and extremely valuable to their firms, simply don't function anywhere near partner level, and their compensation is much lower.

   We used to have a question in The Rosenberg Survey on this statistic. But when we dug down into the responses, we found that many firms responding to the question had a lower-level office manager on board instead of a high-level firm administrator. We never used the data because the results were misleading, so we discontinued the question.

10. **Calculating average fees per professional.** Again, the problem here is one of definition. What is a professional? At some firms, paraprofessionals perform work very similar to the CPAs. At other firms, paraprofessionals are seen as clerical staff. For this reason, we don't place much importance in "average fees per professional." We prefer "fees per person."

Benchmarking Statistics for CPA Firms

The schedules on the following pages contain common CPA firm statistics and ratios, sorted by:

- Annual revenue size of the firms

- Size of the market, as measured by population

- Geographic area of the country

All statistics are from the 2021 edition of The Rosenberg MAP Survey.

How does your firm rate in each category?

The 2021 Rosenberg Survey
Key Statistics and Ratios Using 2020 Numbers
All Groups

MAP statistic	>$20M	$10-$20M	$5-$10M	$2-$5M
Net fees per eq ptr	2,437,830	1,906,064	1,645,417	1,101,949
Net fees per prof	252,358	232,727	228,555	217,131
Net fees per person	206,798	191,877	188,107	179,282
Bill hours – eq ptrs	1,052	1,065	1,163	1,180
Billable hours staff	1,499	1,477	1,508	1,450
Realization %	85.6%	84.6%	87.0%	89.2%
Utilization %	52.1%	52.8%	54.5%	54.8%
Equity ptr bill rate	405	355	334	302
Overall billing rate	183	163	155	148
Ratio staff to eq ptr	9.0	7.3	6.5	4.3
Admin % of total headcount	17.3%	17.4%	17.5%	16.9%
Prof. staff turnover	14.5%	15.6%	15.3%	15.9%
Income per eq ptr	687,739	518,570	504,005	343,495
Pct. incr. in net fees	7.4%	5.9%	6.0%	2.7%
Average size firms:				
Equity partners	19.3	8.6	5.1	3.7
Prof. staff	148.0	55.0	28.5	14.8
Administrative	32.5	13.3	7.1	3.8
Total	199.8	76.9	40.7	22.3
Avg. net fees	40.1M	14.3M	7.4M	3.8M
As a pct of fees:				
Staff comp/benefits	48.3%	49.1%	46.1%	43.4%
Overheads	21.7%	22.0%	22.1%	24.7%
Equity ptr income	30.0%	28.9%	31.8%	31.9%
Overhead exp/prsn	40,666	39,005	38,335	39,070
Services:				
Audit & accounting	42.7%	41.3%	40.3%	39.3%
Tax	38.9%	46.8%	47.6%	48.2%
Consulting	18.4%	11.9%	12.1%	12.5%
Average 1040 fee	1,832	1,337	1,086	920
% w/wealth mgmt	58.1%	32.5%	23.5%	22.2%
% of female partners	18.8%	24.1%	23.7%	33.2%
% w/ non-eq ptrs	88.4%	77.9%	49.0%	27.0%

The 2021 Rosenberg Survey
Key Statistics and Ratios Using 2020 Numbers
Firms >$20 Million in Annual Fees

MAP statistic	2020	2019	2018
Net fees per equity partner	2,437,830	2,543,042	2,339,067
Net fees per professional	252,358	250,675	247,978
Net fees per person	206,798	204,616	200,610
Billable hours for equity ptrs	1,052	1,031	1,034
Billable hours for staff	1,499	1,474	1,448
Realization percentage	85.6%	83.8%	85.0%
Utilization percentage	52.1%	51.3%	50.8%
Equity partner billing rate	405	406	405
Overall billing rate	183	182	178
Ratio of staff to equity partner	9.0	9.3	8.7
Admin % of total headcount	17.3%	17.6%	18.1%
Professional staff turnover	14.5%	18.1%	18.7%
Income per equity partner	687,739	674,711	643,170
Pct. increase in net fees	7.4%	9.1%	9.9%
Average size of firms:			
Equity partners	19.3	18.8	20.1
Prof. staff	148.0	148.0	152.0
Administrative	32.5	33.4	34.9
Total	199.8	200.2	207.0
Avg. net fees of firms	40,139,865	39,233,150	39,535,903
As a pct of fees:			
Staff comp/benefits	48.3%	49.2%	48.3%
Overheads	21.7%	23.3%	24.2%
Equity partner income	30.0%	27.5%	27.5%
Overhead expenses per person	40,666	43,599	45,113
Services:			
Audit & accounting	42.7%	41.1%	41.5%
Tax	38.9%	40.9%	40.6%
Consulting	18.4%	18.0%	17.9%
Average 1040 fee	1,832	2,060	1,936
% of firms with wealth mgmt	58.1%	56.4%	55.9%
% of female partners	18.8%	19.8%	17.5%
% of firms w/ non-eq partners	88.4%	89.7%	82.4%

The 2021 Rosenberg Survey

Key Statistics and Ratios Using 2020 Numbers
Firms $10-$20 Million in Annual Fees

MAP statistic	2020	2019	2018
Net fees per equity partner	1,906,064	1,895,655	1,813,824
Net fees per professional	232,727	233,128	223,868
Net fees per person	191,877	192,214	183,906
Billable hours for equity ptrs	1,065	1,043	1,028
Billable hours for staff	1,477	1,493	1,486
Realization percentage	84.6%	84.1%	85.0%
Utilization percentage	52.8%	52.2%	52.4%
Equity partner billing rate	355	355	343
Overall billing rate	163	163	157
Ratio of staff to equity partner	7.3	7.4	7.3
Admin % of total headcount	174%	17.2%	17.6%
Professional staff turnover	15.6%	16.9%	15.2%
Income per equity partner	518,570	506,375	479,451
Pct. increase in net fees	5.9%	7.7%	9.7%
Average size of firms:			
Equity partners	8.6	8.8	9.0
Prof. staff	55.0	55.1	57.1
Administrative	13.3	13.2	14.1
Total	76.9	77.1	80.2
Avg. net fees of firms	14,292,622	14,256,655	14,261,036
As a pct of fees:			
Staff comp/benefits	49.1%	48.3%	48.9%
Overheads	22.0%	23.3%	23.5%
Equity partner income	28.9%	28.4%	27.6%
Overhead expenses per person	39,005	41,328	39,900
Services:			
Audit & accounting	41.3%	38.1%	42.3%
Tax	46.8%	46.7%	42.7%
Consulting	11.9%	15.2%	15.0%
Average 1040 fee	1,337	1,365	1,288
% of firms with wealth mgmt	32.5%	35.1%	37.3%
% of female partners	24.1%	21.5%	21.9%
% of firms w/ non-eq partners	77.9%	73.0%	78.7%

The 2021 Rosenberg Survey

Key Statistics and Ratios Using 2020 Numbers
Firms $5-$10 Million in Annual Fees

MAP statistic	2020	2019	2018
Net fees per equity partner	1,645,417	1,535,836	1,527,333
Net fees per professional	228,555	229,492	217,797
Net fees per person	188,107	190,269	178,746
Billable hours for equity ptrs	1,163	1,148	1,156
Billable hours for staff	1,508	1,472	1,510
Realization percentage	87.0%	87.8%	87.1%
Utilization percentage	54.5%	53.6%	53.8%
Equity partner billing rate	334	329	318
Overall billing rate	155	153	148
Ratio of staff to equity partner	6.5	6.0	6.2
Admin % of total headcount	17.5%	17.1%	17.7%
Professional staff turnover	15.3%	17.8%	17.0%
Income per equity partner	504,005	477,941	445,604
Pct. increase in net fees	6.0%	5.1%	7.0%
Average size of firms:			
Equity partners	5.1	5.4	5.6
Prof. staff	28.5	28.0	28.8
Administrative	7.1	7.0	7.5
Total	40.7	40.4	41.9
Avg. net fees of firms	7,359,804	7,246,371	7,215,962
As a pct of fees:			
Staff comp/benefits	46.1%	44.9%	44.8%
Overheads	22.1%	23.3%	24.0%
Equity partner income	31.8%	31.8%	31.2%
Overhead expenses per person	38,335	41,012	39,301
Services:			
Audit & accounting	40.3%	40.8%	40.5%
Tax	47.6%	45.3%	45.7%
Consulting	12.1%	13.9%	13.8%
Average 1040 fee	1,086	1,106	1,024
% of firms with wealth mgmt	23.5%	25.9%	33.0%
% of female partners	23.7%	21.9%	23.0%
% of firms w/ non-eq partners	49.0%	52.7%	52.6%

The 2021 Rosenberg Survey
Key Statistics and Ratios Using 2020 Numbers
Firms $2-$5 Million in Annual Fees

MAP statistic	2020	2019	2018
Net fees per equity partner	1,101,949	1,136,669	1,031,407
Net fees per professional	217,131	223,592	216,496
Net fees per person	179,282	184,842	179,102
Billable hours for equity ptrs	1,180	1,163	1,137
Billable hours for staff	1,450	1,448	1,409
Realization percentage	89.2%	89.7%	89.6%
Utilization percentage	54.8%	53.8%	52.0%
Equity partner billing rate	302	303	295
Overall billing rate	148	152	149
Ratio of staff to equity partner	4.3	4.4	4.0
Admin % of total headcount	16.9%	17.2%	17.3%
Professional staff turnover	15.9%	17.0%	16.6%
Income per equity partner	343,495	345,537	332,717
Pct. increase in net fees	2.7%	5.1%	4.8%
Average size of firms:			
Equity partners	3.7	3.6	3.8
Prof. staff	14.8	14.2	14.1
Administrative	3.8	3.8	3.8
Total	22.3	21.6	21.7
Avg. net fees of firms	3,763,748	3,696,360	3,632,006
As a pct of fees:			
Staff comp/benefits	43.4%	42.2%	42.5%
Overheads	24.7%	26.4%	24.3%
Equity partner income	31.9%	31.4%	33.2%
Overhead expenses per person	39,070	44,658	40,474
Services:			
Audit & accounting	39.3%	34.0%	31.6%
Tax	48.2%	50.8%	53.1%
Consulting	12.5%	15.2%	15.3%
Average 1040 fee	920	858	800
% of firms with wealth mgmt	22.2%	30.3%	34.3%
% of female partners	33.2%	31.3%	28.3%
% of firms w/ non-eq partners	27.0%	19.7%	24.3%

The 2021 Rosenberg Survey
Key Statistics and Ratios Using 2020 Numbers
By Size of Market

MAP statistic	Population >2M	1-2M	250K-1M	<250K
Net fees per eq ptr	1,926,757	1,468,935	1,514,622	1,125,902
Net fees per prof	247,275	218,325	202,799	202,927
Net fees per person	204,387	181,059	166,650	166,332
Bill hours eq ptrs	1,103	1,117	1,159	1,216
Billable hours staff	1,490	1,537	1,458	1,446
Realization %	87.4%	86.2%	85.0%	89.2%
Utilization %	54.5%	53.6%	54.0%	53.0%
Equity ptr rate	369	328	303	276
Overall billing rate	173	154	139	138
Ratio staff to eq ptr	7.0	5.8	6.5	4.5
Admin % of total headcount	16.9%	16.3%	17.5%	17.8%
Prof. staff turnover	14.4%	15.5%	17.9%	14.8%
Income per eq ptr	558,822	493,467	441,465	381,800
Pct. incr. in net fees	6.0%	4.2%	5.2%	3.6%
Average size firms:				
Equity partners	6.9	9.6	7.5	6.1
Prof. staff	46.6	63.0	46.5	27.4
Administrative	11.2	12.1	11.7	7.0
Total	64.7	84.7	65.7	40.5
Avg. net fees	12.9M	16.0M	11.4M	6.8M
As a pct of fees:				
Staff comp/ benefits	46.8%	43.4%	47.6%	42.7%
Overheads	22.8%	22.2%	23.1%	22.7%
Equity ptr income	30.4%	29.3%	29.3%	34.6%
Overhead exp/prsn	42,257	39,255	35,382	34,258
Services:				
Audit & accounting	38.4%	41.1%	45.1%	40.2%
Tax	47.8%	41.9%	44.6%	48.7%
Consulting	13.8%	17.0%	10.3%	11.1%

The 2021 Rosenberg Survey
Key Statistics and Ratios Using 2020 Numbers
By Geographic Region

MAP statistic	Midwest	Northeast	South	West
Net fees per eq ptr	1,729,669	1,910,419	1,526,322	1,743,713
Net fees per prof	228,868	241,645	214,181	253,567
Net fees per person	189,271	198,397	178,862	204,161
Bill hours – eq ptrs	1,129	1,151	1,137	1,475
Billable hours staff	1,463	1,568	1,086	1,453
Realization %	87.5%	83.3%	86.7%	90.9%
Utilization %	54.5%	55.8%	54.3%	50.7%
Equity ptr bill rate	331	360	323	337
Overall billing rate	155	163	151	182
Ratio staff to eq ptr	6.7	7.2	6.1	5.9
Admin % of total headcount	17.1%	17.1%	16.2%	19.1%
Prof. staff turnover	15.2%	13.9%	14.8%	17.7%
Income per eq ptr	511,498	523,015	478,623	543,398
Pct. incr. in net fees	4.3%	5.1%	5.0%	8.3%
Average size firms:				
Equity partners	5.6	9.7	7.7	6.9
Prof. staff	34.3	63.2	51.9	37.7
Administrative	8.3	14.8	11.3	10.7
Total	48.2	87.7	70.9	55.3
Avg. net fees	8,854,905	16,933,340	13,148,705	11,508,449
As a pct of fees:				
Staff comp/benefits	45.9%	47.9%	45.9%	44.3%
Overheads	23.2%	23.0%	22.4%	22.8%
Equity ptr income	30.9%	29.1%	31.7%	32.9%
Overhead exp/prsn	40,616	40,759	36,787	42,941
Services:				
Audit & accounting	40.5%	44.1%	41.8%	32.0%
Tax	44.3%	45.2%	45.3%	54.8%
Consulting	15.2%	10.7%	12.9%	13.2%

Geographic regions are composed of the following states:

Midwest: Wisconsin, Illinois, Michigan, Indiana, Ohio, Minnesota, Dakotas, Missouri, Nebraska, Kansas and Iowa.

Northeast: New England states, New York, Pennsylvania and New Jersey.

South: Kentucky, Tennessee, Virginias, Delaware, Maryland, D.C., Arkansas, Louisiana, Mississippi, Alabama, Georgia, Carolinas, Florida.

West: Texas, Oklahoma and all other western states.

Pay Attention to These Benchmarking Metrics

Feeling overwhelmed? Come on, you handle complex tax regulations and perform intricate audit procedures. Surely you can handle a little sophisticated benchmarking.

The four metrics that correlate the most with profitability (as measured by income per equity partner). Whenever we get a new client, the first thing we do, even if we weren't asked to, is perform a quick benchmarking of their firm's key metrics. And the biggest focus of the benchmarking is what we call the big four metrics because these statistics correlate with income per partner (our top measure of profitability) more than any other.

- **Net fees per partner.** This is always #1. It tells us a lot about the firm. Is it over-partnered? Is the bar high enough for promotion to equity partner? Are the partners leveraging their work so they can serve a large client base? Does the firm have a great staff that is well trained to handle high-level work?

- **Net fees per person.** In addition to being one of several measures of leverage, it is a gauge of firm efficiency and productivity. It's a measure of how many people—partners, professional staff and admin—it takes to get the work out.

- **Staff-partner ratio.** Probably the most important of several measures of leverage. When this ratio is high, it is evidence that the partners are good delegators. When this ratio is low, it shows us that

49

the partners hoard staff-level work and that the firm may not be effective at developing well-trained staff (which could be a reason why the partners are reluctant to delegate).

- **Equity partner billing rate.** No one would dispute that a key factor in profitability for most businesses is charging high prices. The same holds true for CPA firms. Strong billing rates are directly correlated with profitability. As I mentioned earlier, they're also an indication of the quality of service provided to clients.

Percentage of Total Headcount That's Administrative

We look at this in two ways:

- If it's above 20% or so, it's often an indication that the firm has too many administration people. Firms sometimes have long-tenured admin people and their productivity often declines as the years pass. In some cases, these people become sacred cows: long-tenured, unproductive people who would be terminated at most other firms, but out of loyalty, the partners just don't have the heart to deal with the situation.

- If it's below 15% or so, that's usually a signal that the partners are doing too much administrative work, which limits their ability to focus on partner-level work. Unfortunately, it may also mean that the firm is too cheap to hire the right number and quality of administrative staff.

Overhead expenses per person. Overhead expenses encompass all expenses except partner compensation, staff salaries and related payroll taxes and benefits. If this metric is too high, it's a signal that the firm is overspending in one or more categories. If this statistic is too low, it often means that the partners are excessively cost-conscious because they see this as a way to boost profitability. Examples include sub-par office space, low spending on technology and virtually no marketing budget. For firm personnel to operate at peak efficiency, they need the proper amount of support.

Percentage of total revenue that is consulting. Firms under $30M report 14-18% consulting. But most of this is really tied to compliance work, mainly handholding: helping recruit a controller, plan for college, apply for a bank loan; answering minor questions on insurance and investments; and a myriad of general questions about running the client's business. By no means am I diminishing the importance of this hand-holding. But it's not really consulting, and that's a direction that firms need to move into.

Most experts anticipate that the market for compliance work in the next 5 to 10 years or so will be flat, or worse, decline. This is mainly due to relentless advances in technology. So CPA firms need to start now to replace their compliance revenue with consulting services such as IT consulting, M&A, business valuations, estate planning, forensics, strategic and succession planning, among many others.

Another important reason for firms to increase consulting revenue is to better satisfy clients' increasingly diverse needs.

Wealth management. Arguably, this relates to the preceding paragraphs on consulting revenue. Here is a real stunner from The Rosenberg MAP survey: Only 22-33% of firms under $20M are providing wealth management services. There certainly are obstacles that hold firms back on this, but the 25% or so of firms providing wealth management experience very strong profits, more so than from their traditional CPA services. Equally important, firms satisfy an important need that clients want.

Average 1040 fee. $1,000 should be rock bottom; I like to see this fee closer to $1,500. Eliminating low-value, small-dollar individual 1040 clients frees up your team to invest more time with high-value clients who prize your services rather than treating you as a commodity.

Percentage of all partners who are female. The national average is in the low 20s. You've got a big problem if this percentage is zero (as in a lot of firms) or 5-10%. Probably 60% of your firm's staff is female. If you can't show female staff that they have a career path to partner, it will be challenging to retain them. A key factor in demonstrating this career path is the presence of female partners as role models. One additional benefit this often provides is they can showcase that raising a family while being a partner is doable.

MP's client production. MPs in our survey chalk up between 661 and 1,061 billable hours and manage client bases of $1.1M to $1.6M. That's way too much client work interfering with their management of the firm. For firms over $10M, the MPs should have no more than 500 billable hours. It takes 500-750 hours a year to properly and proactively manage a CPA firm in this size range.

Percentage of annual charge hours incurred in the tax season. 45-48% is reasonable. Once this gets above 48% and especially over 50%, this means the firm doesn't do a very good job of spreading the work over the year or doesn't have enough work to do outside of the tax season. High percentages in this category means that people are working horrific hours during tax season and then are scrounging for work after April 15. Not good.

Partner compensation method. This was addressed in Chapter 2.

- Objective systems such as primary compensation formulas incentivize partners to do what's best for them, not necessarily best for the firm. And they ignore critically important intangible factors like firm management, staff mentoring, teamwork and loyalty.

- Subjective systems evaluate partners on traditional objective production measures (finding, minding and grinding) *as well as* intangible factors. The two main subjective systems are the compensation committee and the MP-decides approach.

For firms with five or more partners, the most common systems *by far* are subjective systems.

Firms are more successful and profitable when partners excel at both production and intangible performance attributes because the firms are incentivizing partners who do what the firm *needs* them to do.

Member of CPA associations and roundtable groups. The essence of this is that many heads are smarter than one. Among the main benefits of membership in the 30 or so CPA associations in the country or 10 Kuesel/Rosenberg/Rampe roundtable groups are the formal and informal meetings, conferences, email exchanges and other forms of communications. At these sessions, everyone learns from each other. One MP of a $20M firm, who has been a member of our Chicago roundtable for 20 years, has told the group repeatedly: "At every meeting, I learn at least one or two things about managing our firm that I take back to my firm and implement." For the life of me, I don't understand why *any* firm that wants to be successful and increase profitability would not join an association or roundtable or both.

CPA Firms Make More Money
When Partners Do *Less* Billable Work

There is a natural tendency for partners to perform high levels of billable hours, perhaps in the 1,300 to 1,500 range annually. There are several reasons for this:

1. Partners feel they can do the work faster, more accurately and at a higher realization rate than staff.

2. Partners' work often doesn't need to be reviewed.

3. When partners do the work instead of staff, it's charged at a partner billing rate instead of much lower staff rates.

4. It's easier to meet deadlines because you don't wait for staff.

5. Partners' compensation may increase if their billable hours are higher, depending on the system in place.

6. If partners are honest, they *like* doing billable work, regardless of the level of work to be performed.

Three huge problems arise when partners do too much staff-level work.

1. The firm makes less money. That's right, the firm makes more money when partners do *less* billable work. I'll prove this just a few paragraphs below.

2. When partners do staff-level work, they shirk one of their most important duties: training and mentoring staff to help them learn and grow. This can make the difference between a firm having a great staff with upward potential and a mediocre staff with weak technical skills and low leadership potential. When partners hog the work, they spend less time developing staff, which hinders staff growth.

3. The more time partners spend on delegable work, the less time they have for intangible activities such as business development, firm management and developing new services and niches. These non-billable activities are quite a bit more valuable to the firm than billable work.

To prove that firms make *more* money when partners are *less* billable, we went into The Rosenberg MAP Survey Data Laboratory and did some research. We computed the following statistic: Percentage of partners' client base performed by themselves. The fraction is

$$\frac{\text{Partners' billable time (rate x hours)}}{\text{Partners' client base}} = \begin{array}{l}\text{Percent of revenue performed}\\ \text{by partners}\end{array}$$

By George, I think I may have invented a new MAP statistic (as if we need another one)!

I'm going to spare you the boring details and give you the results:

- The percentage of revenue performed by all partners, that percentage ranged from 18-24% of their client bases, depending on the size of the firms.

- For the half of the firms with lower percentage of revenue performed by partners ranged from 12-17%. These firms posted income per partner that ranged from 13-22% *higher* than that of firms with higher percentages.

From a financial standpoint, as measured by income per partner, firms' profits are higher when partners are less billable.

Equally important is the conclusion that partners should err on the side of being less billable so that they focus on developing technical, client relationship, servicing and leadership skills in their staff. The more that partners turn themselves into delegators, trainers, and mentors of the staff, and the less "doing" they do, the stronger their staff will be, making the firm infinitely more successful and profitable.

The hardest thing about benchmarking is taking action, plain and simple. It's easy to review a MAP survey, read this book, compute your own statistics, make comparisons and identify areas where you lag behind industry norms. It's much harder to take action and implement programs to improve performance in key areas. But I know you can do it!

4

Increasing Profitability with Effective Staff Management

"Treat people as they are and they will remain as they are. Treat people as they can be and should be and they will become as they can and should be."

Goethe

If there is a common theme to this book, it's that profitability in a CPA firm isn't achieved by making it a goal. Instead, high levels of profitability are attained *as a result* of doing the right things to manage the firm effectively. Managing staff is certainly at or near the top of the list of those right "things."

Your Staff: A Major Factor in Success and Profitability

If you ask CPA firm managing partners the most important key to the success of their firm, near the top of their list is "our people." There are many reasons for this:

1. Having a staff that is motivated, engaged, skilled, ambitious, productive and personable is critically important. No one would disagree with this. Just ask firms whose staff lack these traits.

2. The CPA firm business has traditionally experienced a high turnover rate. A rule of thumb is that the cost of replacing a staff person ranges

from 1 to 1.5 times a person's annual compensation. So the pain of turnover is compounded not only by the nearly impossible task of replacing the employee who leaves but by its high cost as well.

More importantly, retaining good staff enables firms to ultimately provide better service to clients. When firms become great places to work where staff stay and thrive, client service always improves.

3. At multipartner firms, 70-90% of all client work must be performed by staff. This won't be possible unless firms invest tremendous time and resources into developing staff who can perform the work at a highly proficient level.

4. Firms need a continuous flow of new leaders to grow and success-fully transition work from retiring partners. This will occur only if the firm excels at developing staff.

Advice from Jack Welch

During his legendary tenure at the helm of Fortune 100 giant General Electric from 1981 to 2001, Jack Welch, former chairman/CEO of General Electric, appeared on everyone's list of top 10 CEOs. The accomplishments of GE during his reign were truly spectacular.

Woven throughout the books he authored and articles written about him is Welch's #1 management philosophy: his fanatical insistence that GE executives consistently demonstrate their commitment and *proven success* in developing people. Indeed, he required that the top executives of each business unit identify and develop future leaders. He made coaching, training and developing people a performance metric that carried equal weight to financial results in determining promotions and compensation.

Staff Best Practices

One of our Rosenberg books, *CPA Firm Staff: Managing Your #1 Asset,* (www.rosenbergassoc.com/shop) is entirely devoted to best practices for managing CPA firm staff. Here is a short summary of those practices.

What Staff Like

1. Being with clients. Partners must resist the temptation to monopolize the relationship with clients. They should let the staff work at clients' offices rather than always bringing work back to the office for staff.

2. Young co-workers. When we conduct focus groups of CPA firm staff, we ask them what the best thing is about working at their firms. The #1 factor is "the people I work with."

3. Learning. Staff want to continually build their portfolios of skills and experiences. When they stop learning, they quit to find another job with better opportunities. Make sure your firm has a robust training curriculum.

4. Technology, the more the better. Staff are turned off by firms that are attached to paper and by partners who barely know how to start a video call.

5. Opportunities to give their input into changes in the firm. They like transparency. They like to know that their opinions matter.

6. A firm that's going places. When firms stagnate, they die. It's really cool to work at a firm that is growing and earns a great reputation in the community. Conversely, when firms are stuck in the mud, it's more difficult to retain their better people.

Make sure your firm addresses all of these staff likes.

Flexibility

Staff also like to decide when and where they work. Of course, when the firm is flexible on work arrangements, it's still important that client needs are met and training is effective.

Great bosses

The driving force of this section is that the #1 reason why people leave any company is their relationship with the boss. At CPA firms, guess who the bosses are: the partners, of course. (Certainly, managers are important too, but at many firms, it's the partners that count the most).

Being a good boss has two parts to it:

- Being nice. Upbeat. Caring. Respectful. Courteous. Accessible. Nice bosses are fun to be around.

- Helping staff learn and grow. Being nice is not enough. Just as important is the boss helping staff increase their knowledge, experience and expertise.

Recognition

People crave recognition, though many are reluctant to admit it. When staff work hard and put in extra effort, their supervisors need to recognize their efforts. Financial rewards are important, but in the long run, people want to be acknowledged for their contributions, too.

Perhaps it's the training that CPAs receive over the years in catching mistakes. Perhaps it's their low-key, conservative personalities. Unfortunately, CPAs tend to fall short on giving the proper amount of recognition to their staff. Many egregiously feel that if someone merely does their job, that this doesn't warrant any special treatment or recognition. Practice the most important advice from the best book ever written on management, *The One Minute Manager* by Blanchard and Johnson: "Catch them doing something right."

Mentoring

The essence of staff mentoring is this: The firm doesn't want to leave retention and staff development to chance. It wants to be *proactive* about helping staff learn and grow. At CPA firms where staff often have multiple bosses, it's natural for the staff to wonder "Who's looking after me?"

Effective mentoring doesn't happen because the firm *wishes* it. Like any other major system in the firm, mentoring needs to be formalized and shepherded by a key person in the firm.

- The program is coordinated firm-wide.

- The matching of mentors and mentees is formalized.

- There are requirements for convening mentoring sessions.

- Not everyone can be an effective mentor. Training may be required. Some people shouldn't be allowed to be mentors.

- Goal setting and monitoring of progress is helpful.

The ultimate measure of a mentor's effectiveness is the extent to which they can demonstrate, by name, staff who advanced under their tutelage.

Here is a true story about how *not* to be good mentors.

> I was facilitating a ten-partner firm's retreat. Throughout the day, the partners kept complaining about how disappointed they were in their staff.
>
> After about the seventh time someone uttered this grievance, I said, "Time out. You have been complaining about your staff all day long. I'm tired of hearing this. What are you, the partners, doing to develop your staff?"
>
> This was first greeted by dead silence. Then the oldest partner asked me: "Marc, are you suggesting that we, the partners, should help our staff succeed? No one mentored *us* when *we* were their age. We worked hard and pulled ourselves up by our own bootstraps."
>
> I didn't ask him how long that took and how many mistakes he made along the way. I simply replied, "Yes, a major duty of all partners is to mentor the staff and help them learn and grow."

When mentees are made more effective by the mentoring process, this improves the firm because engaged staff provide better service to clients, are more productive and work better with co-workers. All of these outcomes increase the firm's success—and profitability.

Leadership development

Some believe that certain skills are innate, that people are either born with them or not. You either have them or you don't. Common examples are bringing in business and working smart. Another one is developing oneself as a leader.

I'm here to tell you that these beliefs are dead wrong. People *can* be trained to be leaders. Evidence of this is the substantial amount of time and money that CPA firms spend on both internal and external leadership development programs.

Like many of the desirable attributes in this chapter, leadership skills aren't developed casually. Firms need to formalize their efforts. This is done by providing classroom training supplemented by mentoring and good supervision and by giving the staff real-life experience in managing staff and clients.

Career growth opportunities and challenging work

Studies by the AICPA have shown that of all the issues important to staff, career growth opportunities and challenging work are at or near the top. When these features of a job stop or stagnate, people leave. Bottom line: If you want to retain your staff, you'd better figure out ways to offer them career growth and challenging work. Here are some specific practices that firms offer:

- Define in writing the criteria for advancement from level to level. Share them with the staff in counseling and mentoring sessions.

- Mentor proactively. *Telling* the staff what they need to do to advance is only the first step. Firms need to work with the staff to help them make progress.

- Provide written job descriptions.

- Offer the training your staff need to advance. Not just technical skills, but technology and interpersonal skills as well.

- Stretch your staff. The firm must think of ways to assign staff to progressively more complex work. Vary the type of work and clients assigned to keep staff from feeling that they're in a rut.

- Partners should err on the side of over-delegating.

Compensation

Jack Welch, former CEO of General Electric, said: "If you pick the right people and give them the opportunity to spread their wings and you couple this with compensation as a carrier behind it, you almost don't have to manage them."

For many years, I've been hearing from partners that compensation doesn't matter that much to today's staff. I have yet to see a survey that evidences this. Here's the thing: Compensation doesn't mean much to staff if they don't like the work hours and lack of work-life balance, if the work is boring, if they don't see advancement opportunities and the partners are uncaring bosses.

I like to say that compensation is ante to get into the game. Staff want *both* job satisfaction *and* good pay. This is even more important with today's labor shortages. If you aren't willing to pay your staff an attractive wage, someone else will.

Training

I cringe when I see firms use the terms *CPE* and *training* synonymously. Firms too often consider the former obligatory technical training, usually boring, provided mostly just to satisfy statutory requirements for CPE hours.

Yet training is everything CPE is and a good deal more. Training is proactive, in alignment with what the person needs to do their job and advance in the firm. Training is not just technical accounting and tax; it includes soft skills and technology education.

Again, as we've said throughout this chapter, staff development policies have a direct impact on profitability. It stands to reason that the better your staff are trained, the more effective and productive they will be at performing their work.

Performance feedback

Another of my favorite quotes from *The One Minute Manager:* "Feedback is the breakfast of champions."

It's important to remember one of the most basic purposes of performance feedback: to improve performance. Everyone can improve, even top performers. Even partners! With this in mind, you can quickly see how performance feedback leads directly to increased profitability. If people aren't aware of the areas in which they need to improve, then they will endlessly repeat the same mistakes.

Recruiting

Given the tremendous difficulty firms are having recruiting in a labor market pockmarked with severe talent shortages, it might seem like a blinding flash of the obvious to write about the importance of recruiting.

But there are some things that progressive firms can do to be better at recruiting than their peers:

- Take full advantage of internships, which are the best way to hire people effectively.

- In making your recruiting pitch to prospective staff, be sure to describe your firm in ways that *differentiate* you from other firms.

- Consider a merger. Many firms merge in firms more to acquire talent than to access more revenue and profit.

- Recruiting is not just a job for the HR department. All firm personnel should actively engage in identifying good people to hire. This is especially the case for the managing partner. Steve Jobs said: "Hiring the best is a leader's most important task."

The better job a firm does of recruiting people, in terms of both quantity and quality, the bigger the impact on the bottom line.

Surveying your staff

If I've heard this once, I've heard it a thousand times: I suggest to partners that if they are truly serious about having a great staff, they need to survey what the staff think of the firm, the partners and their jobs. The all-too-common response is both comic and tragic at the same time: "We know what the staff think. We don't need to survey them."

My experience has been that many firms *don't* really know.

If your firm is truly serious about developing a great staff, you need to do a "performance review" of how the firm treats its staff and survey their feelings. Armed with the results, the firm puts itself in a great position to not only make improvements but show the staff how serious it is about making the firm a great place to work.

Teach your staff the business
of public accounting and how the firm works

Engaging your staff by involving them in the business can drive revenue and profits. When you teach your staff how the firm operates and what drives success, they become smarter businesspeople and gain a better understanding of what they can do to help the firm succeed. People in any organization work with more enthusiasm and commitment when they genuinely feel part of the company and understand the business.

It has been my experience that partner groups are much too secretive about the inner workings of the firm and how the staff fit in. I'm not suggesting that partners do anything radical like publicizing their incomes to the staff, but firms can share a lot more information than most of them actually do.

The supreme challenge

Motivated, productive, highly skilled staff will always be a critically important factor in determining a CPA firm's success and profitability. No one could possibly dispute this.

The supreme challenge is getting the partners to *truly* believe this and hold them accountable for how they *act,* every day, to develop staff. These are the obstacles that firms need to overcome:

- Partners are often too busy to make staff development a priority. Many of them always seem to prioritize client matters over staff development activities.

- Despite the partners *saying* that developing staff is critically important, you would be hard-pressed to find this to be a meaningful factor in the allocation of partner income, especially at firms under $20M. You get what you reward. If there is little or no factor in compensation for staff development, it's unlikely that the partners will devote sufficient effort and energy to staff issues.

- Many firms don't have *any* goals for their partners. For firms that *do* have partners' goals, they're often limited to business development, increasing one's client base and performing billable hours. Few firms set goals for intangibles such as staff development.

- Lack of partner accountability is woven throughout the items listed here, but it's important to state it directly. If there are no consequences for partners who fail at developing staff, then it is less likely that they will succeed at it.

If firms truly want to manage their staff effectively, the effort must start with the partners.

5

Increasing Profitability with Growth and Business Development

"You Can't Not Try"

Tactics designed to increase revenue are the best ways to increase profitability. Certainly one of the most obvious ways is by bringing in more business. Firms usually find that a substantial portion of the additional business falls directly to the bottom line.

Marketing and business development are certainly among the biggest, if not *the* biggest, ways the CPA industry has changed over the past 40 years. Many years ago, a client of mine told me that all a CPA needed to be successful was to hang out a shingle and have strong technical skills and reasonably good interpersonal skills. Sooner or later, clients would find their way to the door.

This "wait for the phone to ring" approach to business development may work from time to time, but it's a tragically flawed approach.

Proactive business development—efforts to bring in business—still scares most CPAs. Many labor under the misguided assumption that only a natural-born "life of the party" type can be effective as a business-getter. We totally disagree with this notion.

My work with firms has *absolutely convinced me* that almost everyone can bring in business and enjoy success at it. But they have to *want* to do it. And they must be willing to invest some time in getting training in BD. Business development, just like any other new discipline, requires training, study, persistence and trial and error.

Can the most boring, introverted and impersonal individual be transformed into a rainmaker? Absolutely not. But people can get better. If a CPA's marketing ability is ranked on an ascending 10-point scale, he or she can move from a 3 to a 5, or from a 6 to an 8, and so on. (I'm afraid that little can done with 1s and 2s.) In other words, people who are less talented at BD can move up levels. They *can* get better.

Years ago, I facilitated a retreat for a six-partner, second-generation firm. Their fees had declined for three straight years. We went around the table and each partner stated what they were doing to bring in business. One by one, each of them admitted they were doing virtually nothing. No wonder their fees were declining.

Firms can no longer afford for most or all of their partners to be inactive in BD. Since it's unlikely that the firm will have a rainmaker (most firms don't), the next best thing is to get as many people in the firm, both partners and staff, to generate a little mist.

Many years ago, I heard a speech on this topic by Jerry Atkinson, former managing partner of a successful firm in Albuquerque, a former AICPA chair and a real strategic thinker. Jerry said his firm had a credo that all partners must subscribe to: *"You can't not try."*

This suggests to me that the firm understands that some partners will be better at BD than others. But the firm also understands the importance of getting as many people as possible to *try* to bring in business. It also suggests that partners can contribute in different ways. If some partners aren't effective in generating business, they can contribute by writing articles, giving speeches, organizing client seminars and other methods of promoting the firm.

Best Marketing Practices

These best marketing practices are listed in a general order of effectiveness. However, every firm is unique. What works best for one firm may not work as well for others. This section is excerpted from our book *CPA Firm Growth: Keys to Practice Development*. www.rosenbergassoc.com/shop

1. **Have a vision for growth** because it dictates the scope of your marketing activities. A marketing plan calling for 10% growth will need to be much more intense and aggressive than a plan for 3% growth.

2. **Prime the pump.** Business development cannot be turned on and off as needed. Continuous BD, even when you are busy with clients, is the only way to avoid the lengthy time it takes to ramp up. Remember ABC. Always Be Closing (from *Glengarry Glen Ross*).

3. **Remember that BD is a contact sport**: the more at-bats (sales pitches to decision-makers), the more hits (new clients).

4. **Focus on relationships.** Getting new business is all about relationships. No marketing plan can ever replace the personal touch. People create growth, period.

5. **The best source of new business is your existing clients.**

   - Expand existing services, cross-sell other firm services and receive referrals.

   - Proactively brainstorm with clients to make their business more successful and profitable.

   - Clients are more likely to give you referrals if you provide them with world-class service.

6. **Focus on the 20%** or so of your biggest clients and do *more* for them. Don't ignore the 80%, but don't let them prevent you from providing world-class service to the 20% group.

7. **Manage your time.** Partners need to manage their overall time to be proactive at BD instead of doing it reluctantly in as little of their spare time as they can get away with.

8. **Develop services beyond compliance** to meet your clients' needs and exploit cross-selling opportunities. Great examples:

   - Consulting. Learn to find opportunities for your clients, not mistakes. Understand that clients value good advice that will help them run their businesses more profitably more than they value basic compliance services.

   - Wealth management services.

   Understand that the coming technology disruptions will decrease compliance services dramatically in the next 5 to 10 years. Firms need to be developing plans *today* to replace revenue losses *tomorrow*, especially in audit.

9. **Develop industry niches and specialized services**. This makes marketing and BD infinitely easier. Also, niche and specialty services are more profitable than generalist work.

10. **Analyze your pricing**. Be a lower-volume, higher-price firm, not a high-volume, lower-price operation.

11. **Manage your pipeline**. Part of your marketing plan should be to continually feed your firm's pipeline of sales leads.

    - Identify prospects and follow up with them.

    - Every partner creates an individual marketing plan.

    - Network.

12. **Use a CRM system, preferably one created for the CPA firm industry such as ABLE,** a tool to help CPA firms grow their practice and transition from compliance to advisory services. In addition to CRM functionality, it helps partners and managers keep tabs on their best relationships, maintain a robust sales pipeline, and distribute knowledge and information in a hyper-precise manner. Learn more at www.growwithable.com.

13. **Differentiate your firm** from other CPA firms. It's not enough to *say* you're different. You actually need to *be* different. Get started *today* to differentiate your firm.

14. **Brand your firm.** It's a great way to get name recognition and to differentiate your firm from others. Actively and tastefully promote your firm.

15. **Have a marketing champion.** Every firm needs someone who owns the firm's marketing plan and coaches other firm members to be successful in their marketing and BD efforts.

16. **Provide training** in business development.

17. **Provide mentoring** in BD. Without it, the sales training alone may not be effective.

18. **Offer bonus plans for staff** who bring in business. The bonus plan will not be motivating unless it is coupled with ongoing, proactive sales training.

19. **Impose accountability** for marketing and business development. Goal setting is a must.

20. **Set rules for partner compensation** that treat bringing in business as a big factor in allocating partner income.

21. **Nurture referral sources.** It takes constant care and feeding to maintain existing referral sources and create new ones. Stage referral events on a regular basis.

22. **Implement a marketing plan.** Make your marketing *firm-centric*, not *partner-centric*. Rainmakers are always welcome, but create a *firm-wide* marketing plan to drive all firm activity.

23. **Use blogs, newsletters and social media** to create and enhance your firm's name recognition and establish thought leadership.

24. **Follow up on all marketing and business development activities** designed to identify opportunities: seminars, blogs, newsletters, networking events, direct mail, etc.

25. **Never go on a sales pitch alone.** Embrace team selling. Bring along a staff person to learn from watching you. Or bring along a senior firm member with a different area of expertise to show prospects the diversity of your firm's talent.

26. **Make bringing in business a criterion for partner.**

27. **Start staff as early as possible in business development.**

28. **Polish your elevator speech.**

29. **Join a CPA association** and/or the Association for Accounting Marketing (AAM) to avoid living in a cocoon. Learn from other firms by being with them.

30. **Consider mergers** as a great source of growth.

6

Increasing Profitability with Partner Compensation Systems

I know that some of you are reading the title of this chapter and asking, "What on earth does a firm's system for allocating partner income have to do with firm profitability?" Let me help you understand.

It's all about the adage repeated throughout this book: "As the partners go, so goes the firm." For firms to optimize their success and profitability, the partners must be highly effective. This means partners need to

- Be productive.
- Bring in business.
- Retain clients and help them grow.
- Have decent relationships with each other.
- Be on the same page, adhering to the firm's core values.
- Do the things the firm needs them to do.
- Be accountable.
- Be leaders.

When partners do all of these things *well,* firms are more successful and more profitable. Plain and simple. Conversely, when partners fail to perform partner duties effectively, profitability suffers.

You Get What You Reward

In the field of compensation, "you get what you reward." This means that when certain tasks or duties are linked directly to compensation, it's more likely that these tasks and duties will be performed well. Conversely, the absence of these links often leads to disappointing results or to ignoring the duties and tasks altogether.

The best example of the "get what you reward" maxim is partners mentoring staff, helping them learn and grow and advance under their tutelage. At many firms, if you ask partners what is critically important to their firms' success, they will cite staff development. Yet many of those firms would be hard-pressed to find a meaningful, clear factor for developing staff in their partner compensation system. As a result, at many firms, the partners *say* that staff are critically important but they fail to *act* like it.

Partner Compensation Systems
Must Reward the Behavior They Desire

Here's how partner compensation systems trigger counterproductive behaviors:

- If a firm uses a formula (such as finding, minding and grinding), it encourages partners to build up their metrics, which often causes partners to game the system, which leads to hoarding clients and billable hours, failing to delegate work to staff and discouraging teamwork.

- If a firm handsomely rewards partners who have built up a large client base over many years, this results in a sort of "annuity" whereby partners are practically guaranteed to earn high incomes every year. This leads to coasting. Sometimes coasting is intentional (partners stop trying to build their client bases); sometimes it's subconscious. Either way, coasting can lead to stagnation. And when you stagnate, you die a slow death.

- Firms whose compensation systems rely heavily on traditional production (finding, minding and grinding) don't give enough recognition to intangible performance attributes such as staff development, firm management and teamwork. It's more important what partners do with their *nonbillable* time than their *billable* time.

- If compensation is not used as a measure of partner accountability (though it's not the only measure or even the *best* measure), then firms will experience very little accountability.

- If a firm creates a clearly articulated vision but partners are not rewarded for helping the firm achieve that vision, then the effort to implement the strategic plan will be wasted.

Using Your Partner Compensation System to Increase Profits

1. **The system must be performance-based**. There should be a strong, direct link between partner compensation and performance. Partners need motivation to do what the firm *needs* them to do, so it must reward them. Performance-based systems help the firm avoid stagnation. By contrast, *nonperformance-based* systems like allocating income based on ownership percentage or seniority lead almost inevitably to stagnation.

2. **Income should include at least two primary tiers**:

   a. A base or a draw that recognizes partners' historical performance and street value.

   b. An incentive bonus that compensates partners for their *current-year* performance. The bonus rewards performance that enabled the firm to earn more profits than the prior year.

3. **The system should be primarily subjective instead of objective or formula-driven.** This means that the allocation of income should be determined by one or more people who assess the performance of each partner and allocate income accordingly. The performance assessment should blend traditional production factors (finding, minding and grinding) and intangible factors (staff development, firm management and teamwork, among others). Objective systems limit the judgment used to assess partner performance. Subjective

systems make use of a broad array of performance factors and allow the use of sound, fair judgment by impartial people (either a compensation committee or the managing partner alone).

4. **Coasting should not be rewarded or even tolerated.** The bonus should be large enough to encourage partners to work hard and smart every year. At the same time, partners should not rest on their laurels and be content staying put after building a large client base.

5. **Achievement of goals matters.** One of several ways to assess partners' performance is to measure the extent that they achieved formal, written goals prepared at the beginning of the year or quarter.

6. **Don't overcompensate partners who have high billable hours.** When measuring partners' traditional production, firms should weight their billable hours (grinding) much lower than bringing in business (finding) and the size of their client base (minding). Partners should be pushing down work to staff as much as possible, not doing staff-level work themselves. Firms should not be rewarding partners who spend too much time on billable work because this usually results in inadequate attention to critical nonbillable activities such as staff development and firm management.

7. **Teams are more profitable than solos.** Smaller firms tend to operate as a group of sole practitioners that share a firm name, overhead, admin systems, and staff. This limits their profitability. By contrast, partner groups that operate as a team rather than as individuals usually see great profitability. This needs to be a factor in allocating partner income.

8. **Closed systems are more profitable than open ones.** The premise of this chapter is that when firms have an effective partner compensation system, their profitability benefits. But if a firm operates an open system (every partner knows what all partners earn), the effectiveness and fairness of the income allocation system is compromised. Why? Because it's human nature for those who allocate partner income to be unduly influenced by the partners' perceived reactions to their new compensation.

Here's a classic example. CPA firm partners earn a fantastic income: higher than the vast majority of all jobs, higher than their parents earned by far and greatly exceeding their expectations when they graduated college. As a result, when they see their new compensation as allocated by either the MP or a compensation committee, these partners are very, very happy. They find it hard to believe that they are making so much money.

But then their balloon bursts. They find out that another partner got a bigger increase and/or is receiving total compensation that exceeds their own. If they believe that partner performs at a lower level than they do, now they are livid.

A closed system minimizes the damage.

> *"If people are concerned about their absolute level of compensation, then they can be satisfied. However, if their focus is on relative standing, then they can never be satisfied."*
>
> *Andrew Grove, former chairman of Intel*

So Now What Do You Think?

Now you can see how the use of a proper partner compensation system can have a positive impact on firm profitability. For those of you who shrieked with horror at the title of this chapter, what do you say now?

7

Increasing Profitability
with Pricing

This chapter was provided by Kristen Rampe,
CPA, Partner at Rosenberg Associates.

With the obvious connection between billing rates and profitability, it seems logical that CPA firms could simply raise their rates and be more profitable. I wish it were as easy as that, and it some ways it is, but the challenge in our industry is that many professionals are uncomfortable raising rates and charging what they're worth. Even in inflationary times, when it feels easier or justified to raise rates, many CPAs are coming from behind and need to be more aggressive on their price increases.

First let's take a look at the value you provide your clients. Among many other things, here are a few top value-added traits of CPAs:

1. You stay up to date on all of the regulations, guidelines and best practices so your clients don't have to.

2. You are available and responsive to your clients' needs. If they have a question, you answer it quickly.

3. You proactively advise your clients on strategies to make *their* business or personal situation more profitable.

Second, let's look at the perceived challenges in raising rates:

1. We'll write off the increase before we bill and lower our realization.

2. Clients will leave and we'll lose their revenue.

3. Clients will complain and that makes us uncomfortable.

The most difficult challenges fall into these last two buckets. If clients wouldn't leave or complain, who wouldn't raise prices?

Do Higher Rates Equal Lower Realization?

This one is easy. If you don't intend to charge more for your work, then don't raise your rates. But even if you raise your rates 10% and write off 5%, you're still 5% ahead. Better yet, target keeping your realization for hourly work at or above your current level while raising your rates.

As mentioned earlier, you can't take realization *percentages* to the bank, but you can take *dollars*.

Some Clients May Leave, and That's OK

Most firms that go through the process of reviewing their client list and giving some clients a choice to pay a price that better aligns with the value the firm is providing, find that not many clients leave. Certainly not nearly as many as some catastrophizing partners worry about. In fact, many wish *more* clients would leave than actually do.

But what happens if clients do leave because you increase your prices? Some good things happen. Here are some of the benefits:

- You'll have **more capacity to serve your existing clients,** who are willing to pay for the value you provide. And who doesn't need more capacity?

- You'll have **more capacity to serve new clients that align with your firm's strategic objectives**. Maybe you want to move toward a specific niche client base. Maybe you want to take on only larger clients or only those that need multiple services. Encouraging the departure of low-paying clients makes room for you to achieve your goals, including profitability.

- Your **staff will be more content** working on clients that contribute more to the firm's profitability. Many of your clients who demand a discounted price are also a pain to work with. Ask your team.

Dealing with Pushback on Prices

If you make the wise choice to increase your prices, you may get pushback from some clients. Few CPAs are excited about this prospect, and that's what stops them from increasing their prices to or above industry norms. Most clients, however, will recognize they were getting a deal before and understand that as your practice grows and evolves, it will, as all for-profit businesses should, update pricing on a regular basis.

When clients do push back, being prepared with your response can alleviate the stress this situation causes. Here are some sample phrases you can use as appropriate:

Validate: "I understand your concern ..."

Reaffirm your relationship: "We appreciate having you as a client ..."

Revise the scope: "We're currently providing several services to your company (list them if appropriate). Would it be helpful if we changed the scope of our engagement with you to reduce the cost?"

Share what they can change: "If you were able to provide us your information earlier in the year/in a more usable format, we might be able to adjust the price slightly."

Give alternatives: "There are other service providers that may be better suited to your situation."

Share cost realities: "The market for talented accounting professionals makes it difficult for us to provide services at the prices we have been using over the last several years."

Stand your ground: "Our firm is continuing to grow and evolve, and one of our strategic initiatives is to focus more on _____. That was a factor behind our change in pricing for this year/changing our client mix. We would be more than happy to help transition your account to a new service provider."

Evaluating Your Client List

Reviewing your client list at least every two years gives you the chance to see what clients need to be transitioned out. To do this, create a spreadsheet that includes the following information. Some of it will come from your practice management systems, some of it is evaluative.

1. Client name.

   - If a single client (payor) has multiple entities/sub-clients with your firm, have the billed entity in one column and the sub-entity or engagement in a second. This way you can analyze total client value and individual entity/project value.

2. Client's start date with the firm.

3. Client's annual business revenue or personal income level.

   - Used to assess value provided based on size of the client's business or financial situation.

4. Services provided.

   - Use different columns for each so you can sort and filter easily (Corporate Tax, Individual 1040, Client Accounting Services, Audit, Consulting, etc.).

5. Monthly fees, if applicable.

   - Recurring payments for client accounting services (CAS), bookkeeping, CFO services, or similar.

6. Total client annual fees for last one to three years.

7. Realization.

- OK to include multiple years of fees and realization for additional information

8. Relationship grade

   - A–F, based on how easy or enjoyable they are to work with.

9. Would they qualify as "Friends and Family" clients receiving significant discounts from market rate? (Yes or No)

10. Would they qualify as "Strategic Low Price" clients receiving significant discounts from market rate in exchange for being an important referral source or community investment from the firm's perspective? (Yes or No)

11. Potential new price and % increase.

12. Comment field: Would the client think the new price is fair?

    - Helps determine the level of effort needed in communicating the pricing change.

13. Plan to make changes to pricing.

    - What will you tell them? When and in what format? It's OK to tranche clients into several plan groups, OK to have some where the plan is "no change."

14. Timeline for implementing plan.

Steps 13 and 14 above are where the action takes place regarding your client list. It's where you define what price increases make sense for each client or each tranche of clients. Evaluate the data in all of the previous fields for each client or group of clients individually as well as reviewing your firm's client base overall. Document your plans in items 13 and 14.

Steps 9 and 10 are there to help you keep an eye on the size of these pools of clients. All firms have some free or low-paying clients. Most firms would never get rid of them. The problem comes in when that pool takes up more than a reasonable amount of your and your staff's time. How much is reasonable? You need to decide. But it's definitely not 20% of your client base.

Sample Letter for Increasing Fees

The following sample letter shares a minimum price for a simple service (for example, an individual 1040), though much of the language can be leveraged into other engagements. A phone call would be appropriate for more significant clients or long-term relationships.

Dear _____,

Thank you for being a valued client of _____. We're writing to let you know about a few changes we're making to ensure we continue to provide the best value and best service to businesses and individuals.

One change is that we are actively reducing the number of clients we work with and focusing on delivering higher-value services that benefit our client base.

As a result, we are increasing our prices for our _____ services to reflect the value of the professional oversight, attention to detail and review we bring to the process. For 20XX, our minimum price for _____ is $_____, which includes _____, _____, and _____. Additional _____ may be added on and will be priced according to your specific situation.

We understand that your needs may be better met by a professional who offers lower prices to their clients. If that's the case for you, we suggest you consider one of the following more affordable options: _____ or _____.

If you would like to continue working with us for your _____ and other business needs, we look forward to serving you!

Sincerely,

Your CPA

Value Positioning: Questions to Ask Prospects

When scoping a new project, whether it's for a new client or an existing one, asking the right questions will position your firm in a strong light. This will in turn allow you to charge a price that aligns with the high value you'll bring to the client through your work.

1. Tell me about your business.

2. What are your key priorities, currently?

3. Do you envision any changes in your service needs over the one to three years?

4. What are your expectations for your tax / accounting / audit / _____ professionals?

5. What is the most valuable experience you've had in working with a tax / accounting / audit / _____ professional in the past?

6. Have you had any bad experiences? What were they?

7. If you could wave a wand and have a tax / accounting / audit / _____ problem solved, what would it be?

8. On a scale of 1–10, how important are the following three things to you, related to your tax or accounting professional team? (*These are ratings, not rankings, so they can all be 1's or 10's or they can be different.*)

   - Responsiveness to your calls, messages and requests.

   - Expertise in the _(niche)_ industry and specialized knowledge in _____ (e.g., opportunities for tax planning that may save you money).

   - Knowing the price you are going to pay for services upfront.

   Conversation tip: Often all of the above are very important and the client will rate them all 8's to 10's. At some point you can reiterate this and confidently share that you can meet their needs in these areas.

9. If you had an unlimited budget, what role would you like us to play in your business?

Menu, Fixed Fee and Value Pricing

Firms use a variety of pricing practices to increase profitability. Tax practices vary on whether they charge a fixed price or bill hourly. Audit practices are often priced on a fixed fee and accounting services tend to be monthly recurring fixed fees.

Here are the differences among the different pricing models:

Hourly Billing: You bill your clients for the hours you worked times your standard rates. Write-offs are common in this model, but not in the models that follow.

Value Billing: You charge your clients for the value, in your opinion, of the services you provided. This is typically priced in arrears, after you've completed the work. It may start with hours times rates, but it's often adjusted upwards.

Fixed Pricing: You price a project upfront, and the client accepts (or you modify) the price before you begin work. While it may be subject to scope changes, the fee is otherwise fixed.

Value Pricing: This is a form of fixed pricing, but instead of determining a price by simply calculating budgeted hours times standard rates, the firm determines the project's value to the client (often more than rates x hours) and prices the project accordingly.

Menu Pricing: This type of pricing is a derivation of fixed or value pricing in which the client is provided two or three options with varying levels of service. It allows clients to select the option that they feel would best meet their needs.

Which should you use? There's no one answer that applies to all firms. You need to evaluate what purpose it would serve to change your pricing structure and most importantly, who would be involved in pricing. For many firms, the biggest downfall is allowing partners who struggle to charge appropriately to be in charge of their own pricing and billing. Instead consider team pricing or a committee and always have minimums below which the firm has agreed that no project can be priced.

Many firms are finding success with menu pricing. It takes some investment of time to start thinking about options for our clients, but when you can give them choices, they can select the service level that's best for them. Within each option, your prices should be set at levels that enable you to achieve your desired profitability levels. You'll need to be sure the final prices you offer more than cover your costs and fully reflect the value of your expertise, availability and responsiveness.

8

Increasing Profitability with Mergers

A powerful argument can be made that mergers increase profitability as strongly as any other tactic. Why?

- An immediate and significant increase in revenue, a great deal of which falls to the bottom line.

- Ability to acquire the seller's personnel during a time in our profession when all firms are having difficulty hiring people. Today, many firms are doing mergers to acquire staff more than for obtaining new revenue.

- The merger market has transformed from a sellers' market to a buyers' market, which may translate to paying a discounted price to acquire a firm.

We will elaborate on each of these throughout this chapter.

The Merger Frenzy

For the past 10 to 15 years, there has been a merger frenzy in the CPA profession. This has been caused by several factors:

- Demographics are changing. Baby Boomer partners are nearing or reaching traditional retirement ages in droves. 70% or more of first-generation firms never make it to the second because they suck at succession planning. So owners of these firms are faced with only one exit strategy: sell or merge with a larger firm.

- Buyers have a voracious appetite for growth. It's way cheaper to buy clients than to originate them internally. Not too long ago, 90% or more mergers involved buyers and sellers in the same city market. But for the past 5 to10 years, Top 100 firms who were previously called regional firms have become national. They want to merge in firms in cities throughout the country, making them national firms.

- There is a proven track record of increasing profitability via merger. In fact, many firms have done multiple mergers over time, so they have solid experience in acquiring firms that led directly to increased profitability.

- Due to their double-digit revenue increases, buyers have a tremendous need to increase their personnel headcount. Acquiring personnel via merger offers a solution to the current labor shortage.

Merger Definitions

Before we proceed, let's clarify two terms that are often used interchangeably:

An acquisition occurs when one firm, the buyer, purchases a smaller firm, the seller, for cash, with payments over a finite period of years. There is no question that the buyer is the surviving firm. The vast majority of all transactions commonly referred to as "mergers" are really acquisitions.

A true merger occurs when two firms join forces to form a new company, or a smaller firm joins a much larger buyer. Cash is rarely paid upfront. In most cases, the larger firm is the survivor and controls the new firm. However, in some cases, depending on the players involved, the smaller firm may play an important role in operating the new entity.

Throughout this chapter, we will use the term "mergers" to describe both types of transactions.

How Do Mergers Increase Profitability?

- **Increased revenues**. CPA firms are very much top-line-oriented businesses. This means that the most common and effective way to increase profitability is by increasing revenue. Almost always, a significant portion of the added revenue drops directly to the bottom line. Increasing revenue via mergers is a powerful growth strategy. It's cheaper to buy clients than to originate them internally.

- **Acquisition of talent.** A common refrain for years from CPA firms across the country has been this: "If we could only hire more staff, we could increase our revenues. Unfortunately, due to the labor shortage, we have cut back our business development efforts because if we brought in more clients, we wouldn't have the staff to do the work." Acquiring firms with experienced personnel helps buyers address their labor shortage.

- **Bigger is better.** Year after year, data from *The Rosenberg MAP Survey* shows that the higher a firm's revenue, the higher its profitability. This of course is not guaranteed, but it's highly likely. This is due to several factors. Larger firms

  - Find it easier to attract larger clients.

  - Find it easier (not easy) to recruit staff.

  - Have more resources to spend on technology and professional administrators, having attained a critical mass to do so.

  - Are more likely to provide consulting and specialty services, which are among the most lucrative services that a CPA firm can provide.

- **Better management.** Larger firms are almost always better managed than smaller firms. Buyers see opportunities to use their superior management know-how to make sellers more profitable.

Merger Terms That Lead to
Increased Profitability for Buyers

There are many terms in a merger, some major, some relatively minor. None are unimportant. In this section, we list 16 major terms that, if negotiated properly by the buyer, will go a long way to the buyer's goal of increased profitability.

Before we go further, there is one overarching thing that buyers need to understand if they want a merger to make their firm more profitable. It's best explained with an example. (This is based on a true story.)

> Two firms of about the same revenue size decided to merge. It was a classic merger of equals. Their offices were 20 miles apart, the partners had known each other for many years and enjoyed a high degree of respect and credibility with each other. One firm was strong in tax, the other in audit. One firm had younger partners and the other was somewhat older. One firm did its business development in one cultural part of the metro area and the other marketed to a different segment of the population. It seemed that combining the firms would yield a natural synergy.

> But well into the first year of the merger, the two firms had not really merged. Nothing was done to exploit the reasons why the firms did the merger in the first place. The two firms maintained their separate offices. There was very little communication between the two offices, no sharing of clients and no universal policies and work practices that both firms followed. In other words, the firm operated as two completely autonomous firms. Although they may have merged in form, in substance they operated just as they did before the merger.

What was the problem? Ineffective management. As it turned out, neither firm had a strong managing partner. Although one of the few things the firms agreed on was to make one of the MPs the MP of the new firm, this person was not a strong leader and did almost nothing to implement the merger. So when the firms decided to de-merge three years later, it came as no surprise.

Moral of the story: The easy part of a merger is negotiating terms. The hard part is implementing the merger. Without a champion for the merger who works tenaciously to unite the two firms and achieve the synergistic benefits, it is unlikely that the merger will succeed, making it nearly impossible for the buyer to achieve increased profitability. Mergers work, but only if they are done right.

Here are 16 major merger terms that, if properly negotiated, will increase the success of the merger.

1. **Sales multiple**. Understand that paying a sales multiple of 1.0 times fees for a firm with at least average profitability is a steal for the buyer. Although buyers are still offering one times fees in certain circumstances, mainly if the seller is an "above average" firm, the sales multiple has been declining in recent years. Many deals are now going for 75-90% of revenue. Obviously, the less you pay for a firm, the easier it is to make it a profitable investment.

2. **Payments to seller based on collections, not billings.** This is universal. No buyer should lock itself in to a sales price if there is uncertainly that the revenue will be realized.

3. **Down payment**. Sellers love it; buyers hate it. The way the math works in present-value calculations, the more cash is paid in the early years of the merger, the lower the return on investment (ROI).

4. **Seller's transition efforts.** As we have said many times, the only reason a firm should pay for a client base is if the clients stay with the firm. The seller must proactively work with the buyer to transition the client relationships and the work to increase the odds that clients will stay. To make this happen, buyers should require the seller to remain with the firm for two to three years. It may not need to be full-time after the first year. Merger terms should provide for a reduction in payments to sellers who leave the firm before this period is up.

5. **Payout term.** Most deals are four to five years, some longer. Again, the way present-value calculations work, the more cash is paid in the early years, the lower the ROI.

6. **Compensation reduction to the sellers.** In the vast majority of cases, sellers' infrastructure (technology, quality and quantity of staff, training, marketing, admin professionals, etc.) is well below that of the buyers. Initially, buyers will never earn what the seller was earning because costs are higher. Also, in the first year or two,

the buyer will incur start-up costs that further reduce the seller's profitability. To enable the buyer to earn a targeted level of profitability, it is common to reduce the compensation to the seller.

7. **Trust your gut.** One of my favorite sayings is this: "The best way to solve a problem is to avoid it becoming a problem in the first place." Firms should never make someone a partner if they don't feel good about it and if they don't trust their prospective partner. The same criteria should be used for doing a merger. If you don't feel in your gut that the merger is right and that you will be able to achieve your goals for it, *then don't do it.*

8. **The seller's staff is critical.** Everyone knows that we work in an environment where there is an awful labor shortage. Many times, when I first call buyers to see if they are interested in a seller I am representing, their first question is "Does the seller have staff who will come over, and are they any good?" Many firms have told me that acquiring staff in a merger is more important to them than added revenue.

9. **Non-solicitation agreement for staff.** As stated throughout this chapter, two of the biggest factors that lead to increased profitability from a merger are that the buyer adds revenue (clients) and staff. Obviously, buyers and sellers alike will be very unhappy if the seller's staff refuse to join the buyer. Making matters worse is when the seller's staff takes clients. This is addressed by getting the sellers' staff to sign non-solicitation agreements.

10. **Sellers come in as equity partners?** Most buyers have standards for making equity partner that are much higher than the sellers'. Put another way, many equity partners at sellers would never qualify as equity partners at the buyer. Buyers need to avoid overcompensating the sellers' partners who join the buyer. In many instances, they do not join as equity partners.

11. **Part-time compensation for sellers.** It's common that partners want to continue working part-time after they "retire." Virtually all firms pay their part-time retired partners 35-40% of their collected billable time, with no pay for nonbillable time. Don't overpay partners for part-time work.

An exception is the case where a dominant, usually founding partner of the seller gets paid more than the above. This recognizes that this person impacts the success of the firm in many ways *other than* billable hours. In such a case, the compensation is negotiated.

12. **Exit date for sellers' partners.** I have seen many, many cases over the years where the buyer failed to pin down with crystal clarity how long the sellers' partners would be allowed to work and when their exit date would be. In most of these cases, it doesn't turn out well for buyers because they don't want to deal with the conflict of telling sellers who want to keep working indefinitely that they have to retire. It's critical that merger terms specify when the sellers will retire. Buyers' profitability may be impaired by compensating sellers who are unable to perform.

13. **The sellers' office lease.** In most cases where sellers have several years to go on their office lease, the rent involved is quite significant. Buyers are rarely willing to absorb the sellers' lease if the office isn't needed. And sellers usually can't afford to pay rent on an office they don't need. So unless there are significant profit opportunities to the buyer from other aspects of the merger that will exceed the rent, buyers almost never agree to take on the sellers' office lease where unused space is involved.

14. **Beware of sellers' hidden perks.** Here's another example of solving a problem by not letting it surface in the first place. Smaller firms are often operated as extensions of their owners' personal lives. This is a code language for sellers running personal, non-business items through their firm. Examples (that I'm sure you're all familiar with) are country club dues, sports tickets, multiple cars, vacation expenses often disguised as conferences and many more.

As part of the due diligence process, buyers need to request sellers to list all personal items that are included in the expense section of their income statement that will not continue after the merger. It's much easier to deal with the impact of this issue *before* the merger is consummated than after. If this issue is not addressed until *after* the merger, the buyer is put in the awkward position of accepting or rejecting the seller's request for reimbursement of perks.

15. **Buyers: Don't ever tell sellers that nothing will change.** Buyers are usually anxious to sell sellers on the benefits of merging. One thing that is often part of the buyer's sales pitch is assuring the seller that nothing will change. They should expect to continue doing everything they did *before* the merger the same way *after* the merger.

This is an egregious mistake. If the buyer is better managed than the seller and has better policies and processes, the buyer would be a fool for not making changes to the seller. Obviously, if the seller has been assured that "nothing will change," it will be harder for the buyer to initiate these changes, which most certainly are designed to increase the success and profitability of the combined firm.

16. **De-merger clause.** This final item is all about the adage "Attitude is everything." If you don't have a positive, proactive attitude about embarking on *any* business endeavor or work assignment, then your performance will likely be negatively impacted. Implementing a merger is a difficult, complex process that takes several years to accomplish fully. If the seller doesn't have the right attitude about making the merger work, then it may not be successful.

    Virtually all mergers avoid de-merger clauses in their merger agreements because the buyer feels that the presence of such a clause will reduce the seller's commitment—both consciously and subconsciously—to pursing the merger goals to the fullest. If the seller approaches an assignment with an attitude of "if I don't like the task or agree with the policy, I can always leave and unwind the merger," the assignment will not be carried out with the tenacity and commitment required.

Do Mergers Work?

I get asked this question all the time. My response is always the same: "Yes ... if you do them right."

Doing them *right* includes many, many things. Paying attention to the 16 items in the previous section is a great start to making your merger work and increasing your profitability.

9

Partner Relations: Happy Partners Are Productive Partners

"When a corporation says move left, everybody takes a step left. In a partnership, when you say move left, three people go to the bathroom, four people move right and five people leave the firm."

Richard Ungaretti
MP, Ungaretti & Harris

In CPA firms, as the partners go, so goes the firm. The partners bring in most of the business, manage most of the client relationships and engagements, develop and mentor the staff and manage the firm. If the partners don't perform these functions effectively, it is virtually impossible for the firm to be profitable and successful.

When the partners don't get along with each other or don't communicate well, major schisms develop that cause a lack of partner collegiality and cohesion. Work stops being enjoyable. When partner relations and communications are weak, two things usually happen: partner productivity declines, and the firm's ability to resolve problems and implement strategic initiatives all but disappears.

Here is a situation I experienced at a seven-partner firm where partner communications were weak: I interviewed all the partners one on one. I asked each what they are doing to bring in business. One said: "My partners aren't doing business development; why should I?"

Ultimately, the lack of partner cohesiveness takes its toll on the staff. They see what's going on and find it unpleasant to work for a firm where the partners don't get along. Morale declines, cliques evolve and eventually staff leave. It's a vicious cycle.

Call Me Now or Call Me Later

Not too long ago, there were two national consumer product companies that used this promotional theme: "Call me now (to look over your appliance and make sure it won't break down in the future) or call me later (after the appliance breaks down)."

The same holds true in the area of partner relations and conflict. One of the best ways to avoid problems in partner relations is for the partners to agree, *up front*, what the rules of the game are and how they will communicate with one another. Many firms incorporate these as part of their core values. They need to discuss and agree upon issues such as these:

- What is our vision? What should the firm's goals be?

- How much money do we want to make? How hard do we want to work for the money? How satisfied are we with the compensation we're earning now?

- What is a fair way to allocate income among the partners?

- How will the firm be managed? Do we need or want a managing partner? What will this person's authority be? Do the partners want to "report" to the MP?

- How will we get new business? Whose responsibility is it to get it?

- What do we expect of each other? What roles should we each play in the firm?

- What values do we agree on?

- Should our partners be accountable in any way for their performance and conduct?

- How should we bill and collect? How frequently? What are the partners' obligations here?

- To what extent are the partners willing to standardize basic work procedures?

Partner Collegiality vs. Accountability: Can't We Have Both?

CPA firms have gradually realized that to be successful, a firm must manage itself like a *real* business. As firms have pursued this, they have found that they must impose a certain level of partner accountability to achieve the firm's goals. But in the process, many report feeling a diminished sense of collegiality among the partners. Does this accountability need to come at the expense of collegiality?

Not if you do it right. Here are some examples:

1. **Everyone needs to be on the same page.** Partners should take the time to meet outside of the office and talk about their vision for the firm and where they would like it to go. Clarifying the direction of the firm gets everyone pulling together in the same direction. It also provides the firm with the opportunity to draw a line in the sand. Partners who vehemently disagree with the firm's agreed-upon vision should leave the firm or be isolated so they don't prevent the others from pursing the united vision.

2. **Different people produce at different levels.** It's a fact of life that not all partners are created equal. They are not equal in ability and they are not equal in work habits. If the partners understand this and accept it and adopt a performance-based compensation system that accommodates these differences, there will be less anxiety.

3. **Don't overstate the value of current production.** Consider this scenario, expressed by a concerned partner: "I know I'm doing well now, but I'm still worried. This has become a young person's game. What if I can't keep up the pace? How's the firm going to treat me

when I'm older?" Firms must clarify how they take care of older partners so that these people know they'll receive the benefits they've earned over many years with the firm.

4. **Partnership doesn't mean "management by committee."** No organization can be managed effectively by committee. Partners need to understand that they don't have an inalienable right to participate in all decisions. They should delegate most decision-making authority to a centralized management structure, thus enabling them to focus on performing the two main duties of a partner: taking good care of their clients and helping the staff learn and grow.

5. **Everyone needs some rope.** Strong firm management is not synonymous with micromanaging. Collegiality is hard to maintain when partners feel someone is constantly and excessively watching over everything they do.

6. **Conflicts arise when these issues are not addressed up front.** If firms create the proper *structure* for establishing accountability, then conflicts are minimized and partners can be as collegial as ever.

Pick Your Partners Right to Begin With

What characteristics do you want someone to possess before you invite them to be a partner? Leading firms across the country generally choose from the following:

1. Trust. Integrity. Honesty. Sound ethical behavior and judgment.

2. Credibility with partners and staff.

3. Active in business development.

4. Productive; acceptable levels of realization; strong work ethic.

5. A delegator.

6. Manages client relationships effectively; earns client confidence. Grows the firm's revenue to clients.

7. Loyalty and commitment.

8. Team player.

9. Strong communication and interpersonal skills.

10. Leadership skills.

11. Reasonable amount of technical competence.

If your partner group hasn't dedicated time at a retreat to discuss what it means to be a partner and what is expected of a partner in your firm, you may want to consider doing this very worthwhile exercise. I've heard that sometimes after they discuss the qualities partners should have and write them on a flipchart, one partner says, "Oh, no! None of us qualifies to be a partner!"

If firms pick their partners intelligently to begin with—people whose values, goals and capabilities are compatible with those of the existing partners—they will minimize conflict down the road.

Know When to Stay Together and When to Part

Sometimes a parting of the ways is best because the partners are simply incompatible. People change. Their values change. Their priorities may change. In cases where firms have experienced continuous, robust growth, sometimes the firm outgrows a partner. When these changes become so huge as to produce constant conflict, it may be best to shake hands and part ways.

What does it take for partners to stay together? Here are some critical requirements:

Congruity of goals. What are the partners' goals in areas such as firm profitability, personal earnings, growth rate, services to offer, industries to serve, consulting to be provided, training, management structure, long-term strategies and more? These are critically important issues. Compatibility of the partners' goals in these areas and their prioritization is critical not only to a firm's success and profitability but to partner harmony as well. Without goal congruity, it's virtually impossible to avoid major partner strife.

Congruity of values. What are the partners' values in these areas?

- Work ethic.
- Work quality.
- Service quality.
- Fiscal prudence.

- Leadership.

- Work-life balance.

- How decisions are made.

- Importance of staff vs. clients.

- Honesty in dealing with partners and other personnel.

- Teamwork; helping each other out.

- Diversity.

- Commitment to using the firm's technology.

Partner compensation. In allocating partner income, do they agree on the relative weight of the four main performance factors: finding, minding, grinding (billable hours) and intangibles (teamwork, loyalty, mentoring staff and firm management)? How important are things like technical proficiency and seniority?

The partner compensation system is the most sensitive area of firm management. For the compensation system to succeed, most of the partners need to feel that it is reasonably fair. Few partners will remain with a firm if they feel their compensation is unfair compared to that of other partners.

Partner retirement. Most firms agree that retiring partners should receive payment for the value of their interest in the firm. But how much should the retirement payments be? Do the older partners' views of this vary from those of the younger partners? Partner retirement benefits represent a significant unfunded liability to most firms; unless there is agreement on this issue, few firms can surmount this obstacle. Many firms break up as the partners approach the age when the reality of making retirement payments starts sinking in.

Trust. If you can't trust your partner, you have no business being that person's partner. Plain and simple. Integrity, honesty and morality have to be nonnegotiable conditions for harmonious and rewarding relationships among partners.

Communication

To build strong partner relations, there is no substitute for effective communication, on many levels. For a CPA firm, the following steps promote communications that foster effective partner relations:

1. Partners regularly meet with each other on a *formal* basis. These are primarily regular partner meetings and annual partner retreats. Caveat: As firms grow to 10 or12 or more partners and have a strong, active executive committee, many firms do away with monthly partner meetings and move to quarterly.

2. Partners regularly meet with each other on an *informal* basis. If you have children, you know what it's like to come home from a long workday and ask an eight-year-old how his day was. The inevitable response is an unsatisfying variation on "fine." Partners are somewhat similar. Partners need to find time to spend with each other to learn about what's going on with each other, both professionally and personally. Common ways to do this are over breakfast, lunch, drinks after work and ad-hoc chats at the water cooler. Getting together informally in such settings is the best way to forge deep, trusting, caring relationships. These informal meetings are important supplements to the formal meetings.

3. Partners agree on what is expected of *all* partners as well as each partner individually. A set of core values helps with this, but it's worth the effort to create these values only if the partners do not allow transgressions.

4. People should make their partners aware of the personal issues, both good and bad, that their families are dealing with. When partners know about each other's personal and family issues, they are much more sensitive to how these issues impact their performance and conduct at the firm. It's not necessary, and in some cases not appropriate, for partners to share intimate details of certain matters. But in general, sharing of personal information is conducive to good relations.

Conflict Resolution

CPA firm partners have a natural tendency to avoid conflicts with each other, hoping the conflicts will go away by themselves. But Dr. Ellen

Rosenberg says: "Sweeping problems under the carpet only creates lumps." Sooner or later, the partners will stumble over these lumps.

Firms that don't deal with conflict are often paralyzed when it comes to taking any form of action to improve the firm.

I once worked with a firm on a partner relations project that had a severe, unresolved conflict. One partner on occasion shortcut the firm's quality standards. Another partner was greatly troubled by these transgressions. The two got into a major shouting match at a partner meeting. For the next ten years, these partners literally never talked to each other. It's really too bad that the other partners didn't have the courage to resolve the matter.

Ken Kaye, a Chicago-based specialist in conflict resolution, says, "Research has shown that when partners avoid conflict with each other, they enjoy their involvement with the firm less. Partners who think conflict avoidance is the best policy are mistaken. Partners should learn to address conflict, welcome it, and use it as an opportunity to grow. Two heads are better than one only if they can disagree."

Health and Psychological Issues

Health. Partners at firms have a natural tendency to look at themselves strictly in a business context. But the health of the partners plays a huge and generally unappreciated role in their conduct and productivity.

To be successful, partners need to bring in business, charge a certain number of billable hours, manage client relationships effectively and mentor the staff, among many other things. *They also need to take care of their physical and mental health.* Psychologists call this "self-care."

It's the seventh habit of Stephen Covey's *7 Habits of Highly Effective People.* He calls it "sharpening the saw." Partners need to attend to their health needs. This includes eating nutritiously, exercising regularly, attending to medical problems with appropriate medical personnel and finding spiritual renewal through supportive, inspirational sources.

Current family situation. Partners need to be aware of issues that their partners are facing at home. Going through a difficult time with a spouse or child or having a family member face serious health problems can be debilitating.

Owners need to be sensitive to these situations with their partners because they're likely to affect the entire firm sooner or later. Partners experiencing these problems need to share this information so that their colleagues can better understand what they're going through and perhaps offer some help and support. That's one thing partners are for.

Balance of work vs. personal time. "Work-life balance" is one of the buzz phrases of our time. This issue can cause problems when workaholic partners feel that if they put in long hours, sacrificing their personal life, then the other partners should do the same. This kind of attitude and behavior almost always leads to partner conflict.

It's important for each partner in the firm to decide how much and how hard they want to work. The partners as a group need to devise a compensation system that accommodates these variations in work ethic. If one partner wants to work 300 *more* hours a year than the others, and the result of that extra work produces incremental bottom-line results, then that partner should be suitably rewarded.

If another partner wishes to work 300 *fewer* hours a year than the others, and the result is a reduction in that person's contributions to the firm's success and profitability, this person should be willing to accept lower compensation.

In both cases, the reward should be the results, not simply working more or fewer hours.

Never overlook the importance of job satisfaction. The vast majority of people change jobs frequently during their careers. Young people graduating college today are expected to change their *careers,* not just their jobs, multiple times in their lifetime. Why do CPA firm partners think they are any different? Is there something inherently unique about their profession that makes them naturally immune to job boredom or the desire to make a change every now and then?

This is where partner retreats can play a big role. Every few years at an annual retreat, the partners should openly and freely discuss their jobs and their level of satisfaction with them. They should be given the opportunity to modify their jobs and their roles within the context of the firm's overall strategic plan and operating philosophy. This opportunity to make periodic changes to their job in order to sharpen the saw is critical to many partners to keep functioning well.

10

The Strong Link between Partner Accountability and Profitability

The "A" Word in Practice Management

Accountability is a word that strikes fear (unnecessarily, I might add) in the hearts of many partners. We see the problem constantly in the free-agent age of professional sports. An athlete signs a lucrative, long-term contract and promptly starts producing less.

Partners in firms are no different. The worst thing about the partnership form of organization (here's a paradigm if there ever was one) is that it breeds a belief that once they become partners they can do whatever they please, whenever they want. All accountability stops. They adopt the attitude, "I'm a partner and I don't need to be supervised."

I have developed a saying about accountability: "If there are no consequences to failing to achieve one's goals and meet performance expectations, then those goals and expectations are less likely to be achieved."

In discussing the topic of accountability, many partners claim that one of the reasons they *are* partners is that they have reached the stage in their career when they are self-motivating. They don't need any outside forces to hold them accountable. Does anyone *really* buy this? If this were true, then you would get no arguments from me, or any CEO, against abolishing all forms of accountability.

The simple truth is that it is human nature to relax or underperform when no one is watching, when we get paid the same regardless of whether we meet expectations or disappoint our colleagues. We all need external motivation.

Here's another myth debunked: Accountability is *not* best achieved by using threats and negative, punishing behavior. The best approach is for the partner group as a whole to decide how accountability is to be achieved and to let the partners individually suggest the targets and behavior for which they will be held accountable.

The key is to get this all agreed *up front*. Most of the problems associated with accountability occur when it is unclear what the performance expectations are. Arguments ensue because there is disagreement about what was expected. To the extent that the means of accountability are established up front (i.e., the rules of the game are made clear), partner collegiality is actually *enhanced*.

Ten Time-Tested Partner Accountability Measures

Here are the best ways to achieve partner accountability. Every one of these measures is time-tested and works well. Some work better for some firms than others. The key is to not simply provide for the accountability measure, but to *do it well.*

1. **Managing partner "meeting" with partners as necessary**. Of all the items listed here, these opportunities for "attitude readjustment" have the most potential for getting *results*. But it takes a very strong, effective MP, which many firms don't have.

2. **Compensation**. This is easily the most common form of partner accountability, but it is usually not the most effective. Firms reason that the only accountability *measure* necessary is partner compensation because they think that's the most important thing to partners. Partner compensation often has an initial impact on performance, but it wears off after a while.

But when a partner knows that meeting expectations will impact compensation, that partner will likely be more motivated to perform effectively.

3. **An agreed-upon firm vision and strategy**. In his legendary book *Good to Great* Jim Collins wrote: "Before great companies figure out where to drive the bus (strategic planning), they first need to get the right people *on* the bus and the wrong people *off* the bus." According to Collins, "You need executives who argue and debate—sometimes violently—in pursuit of the best answers, yet, on the other hand, unify fully behind a decision, regardless of personal interests."

    It's OK for partners to disagree on the firm's vision and strategy, but the outliers must ultimately be able to accept the vision the group decided on and adhere to it as though they had suggested it themselves. Holding partners accountable for accepting, supporting and implementing the firm's vision is critical.

4. **Peer pressure**. Partners sometimes make the mistake of putting all of the burden on the managing partner to deal with partner performance and behavior issues. Peer pressure from assorted partners can be very powerful, just as it is for children.

5. **Partner goal setting.** If partners are to be accountable, they need to know with crystal clarity what they are accountable *for*. That's where formal, written goal setting helps.

6. **Living and breathing the firm's core values**. When the partners agree on the firm's core values and are held accountable for carrying them out (no transgressions allowed), they are powerfully motivated to perform.

7. **Partner evaluations (written).** Written evaluations are how management communicates with partners to clarify the extent to which expectations were met. Most corporate executives have their performance reviewed periodically by their superiors. Why should CPA firm partners be exempt from partner evaluations?

8. **Surveys of client and staff evaluations of the partners.** This addresses whom the partners are accountable to. Too many firms focus entirely on partner accountability to the *firm*, but partners should be accountable to clients and staff as well.

9. **Clarity about the roles of each partner.** The two main ways to clarify expectations are via written goals and defining each of partner's role in the firm. For example, one partner's role may be to bring in business and delegate the work to others, focus on medical practices and train the firm's personnel on bringing in business. Another partner's role may be to train staff on leadership, be the one partner in the firm who the staff are comfortable talking to and specializing in business valuations.

10. **The door.** The ultimate form of partner accountability. When all the other nine measures fail, the last resort is to ask the partner to leave. This takes a lot of courage and is something most firms are reluctant to do except in egregious situations.

Effective mechanisms for strong partner accountability lead directly to higher levels of firm profitability.

11

Other Ways to Improve Profitability

This chapter gathers 20 ideas for increasing your firm's profitability that go beyond those discussed so far in this book. It also analyzes nine tactics that many people think will increase productivity but that rarely do. This should help you focus on the most effective approaches.

More Proven Ways to Improve Profitability

1. **Hire a firm administrator (or COO).** This strengthens the firm's management in two important ways:

    - It keeps the partners away from administration so that they can focus undistracted on the two main jobs of a partner: taking care of client matters and mentoring staff. (Remember that management is different from administration. Management is about leadership, envisioning, holding people accountable, executing strategy, growing revenue, increasing profits and more. Administration focuses on the day-to-day, operating systems, reporting results, maintaining policies, supporting the firm's personnel and more.)

    - It enables the firm's administration to be performed more effectively than if done by the partners. This occurs because firm administrators (a) have experience performing the job that the partners don't have (though most partners will never admit it!) and (b) are not distracted by client matters, enabling them to make *the firm* their #1 client 24/7.

Partners are paid a lot more than firm administrators: partners across the country average north of $500,000 per year, and most firm administrators earn $75,000 to $175,000. For good reasons. Partners are high-level executives, owners and entrepreneurs who generate and maintain substantial amounts of revenue, possess high levels of technical expertise, manage client relationships, play leadership roles in many areas, especially developing staff, *and* manage the firm. This commands a higher level of compensation than the work of a firm administrator. Therefore, it makes no sense to pay a partner to do the work of a firm administrator.

2. **Establish billable hour targets for all personnel and communicate them to partners and staff.** Monitor actual vs. target hours, focusing on what can be done to help people achieve their goals rather than on beating them up when they fall short. When people know what is expected of them, they tend to be more productive than when they don't.

3. **Keep in touch with lost clients; they may consider coming back.** Many clients leave for greener pastures but become disappointed at what they find there.

4. **Teach your staff the business of public accounting: how CPA firms operate, how they achieve success and how they make money.** A former president of Ford lectured to 50,000 employees on this topic during his career. The MP of a $10M firm had these things to say about a presentation he delivered to the staff:

   - "We know that staff didn't understand how CPA firms work."

   - "Often, staff are focused on the *what*. But the more we can teach staff the *why*, the more energized they become."

One staff person said of the presentation: "I learned the metrics used to evaluate the firm, what my work is worth to clients and how partners bill. This knowledge gives me a much better view of how staff fit into the firm."

Isn't this worth doing at your firm?

5. **Have your administrative staff make (soft) collection calls.** Partners don't like making collection calls, and they may not be as effective as staff in this task. Remember the maxim of collections: "If you don't ask, you don't get."

6. **Your firm should belong to managing partner and firm administrator roundtable groups.** Don't be provincial. Avoid re-inventing the wheel by learning how other firms do the same things you do. The wisdom you can gain from learning how other firms operate is incalculable.

7. **Raise billing rates if realization exceeds 92% or so.** A trick question in the realm of benchmarking is this: What realization rate would result in a grade of A? The knee-jerk response is 100%. But it's the wrong answer. If your realization is anywhere near 100%, this usually means your clients are paying your bills without any pushback, which means your rates and fees are too low

   The root of this issue lies in the fact that different clients have different thresholds of what they are willing (and able, in the case of nonprofit clients) to pay. One group of clients will pay anything you bill. Another group may push for fees that are 10% lower. Still another group will pressure you to go down 20%. And so on. Your overall firm realization percentage is a melding of all of these scenarios. But if all of your clients are paying your bills or accepting all of your fixed-fee proposals without pushback on fees, that usually signals that they are content with what they are paying. This may sound a bit masochistic, but you *want* some of your clients to give you a little (the operative word is "little") grief about your fees.

   In a recent edition of The Rosenberg MAP Survey, the average national realization ranged from 85-89%, depending on firm size. This indicates to me that the optimal realization is probably somewhere between 90% and 92%.

8. **Devise internal procedures for challenging write-offs above a certain dollar amount.** This establishes accountability for billing. If there is no monitoring, some of your partners will write off fees without any justification to avoid conflict with clients.

9. **When administrative staff work on *specific* clients, they should bill their time.** I've heard some partners object to this because they

feel their standard billing rates take into account overhead expenses, which include administrative staff time. This is nonsense.

10. **Eliminate the word *busy* from your firm's vocabulary.** How often have you or your partners said, "I'm too busy" to the following questions: Why are we so slow at following up on leads? Why has no one in the firm devoted more than 50 hours a year to marketing? Why don't we have time to mentor the staff? Why haven't we developed consulting services? What's stopping us from specializing? Why are we so late in sending out bills and collecting receivables? Why don't we have partner meetings more often? Why are the internal financial statements three months late? Why did it take us a month to place an ad in the paper to replace the last staff person who left?

Every one of these issues has a direct impact on firm profitability. How can partners be too busy to do these things? The answer is poor time management and a lack of adherence to the best practice of "doing first things first."

11. **Understand the differences among leadership, management and administration.**

    a. These *leadership* activities are worth *more* than your billing rate:

    - Identify challenges and focus people's attention on them.

    - Constantly find new things the firm needs to be doing, stretching everyone's abilities and imagination.

    - Foster collegiality; build a strong culture and team spirit.

    - Satisfy people's basic human needs.

    - Develop real convictions over time and match them with people who will follow.

    - Solidify the future value of the firm.

    b. These *management* activities are worth your billing rate:

    - Decide what you want to be (plan) and make it happen (implement).

    - Put first things first after leaders decide what those "first things" are.

- Help firm personnel realize their potential.

- Influence the behavior of the partners; establish partner accountability.

- Leverage time by pushing down work to the lowest level that can competently do the work.

- Solve problems swiftly.

c. These *administrative* activities are worth *less*, often far less, than your billing rate:

- Focus on the day-to-day running of the firm.

- Monitor and report operating results (keep score).

- Operate, maintain and upgrade systems.

- Create, enforce and interpret policy.

- Support practice personnel by providing them with an efficient, comfortable work environment, thereby enhancing their productivity.

When partners say they are too busy to do partner-level activities, it often means that they aren't managing their time well and/or doing first things first. Better time management and a keener focus on the most valuable use of your time will directly affect firm profitability.

12. **Terminate Clients**. For decades, one of the techniques that virtually all material on CPA firm management and MAP conference speakers have recommended is to periodically evaluate the profitability and desirability of each of your clients and terminate the undesirable ones. This allows partners to spend more time working on the firm's better clients and looking for new clients who are more profitable and desirable.

I used to use the term "fire" clients until I heard about a firm that doesn't fire clients. Instead, they help their undesirable clients find another CPA firm that can better serve their needs. Firing clients creates ill will for your firm; you don't want all of your "fired" clients out on the street, bad-mouthing your firm.

Instead, strike up relationships with two or three small firms in your community that you don't see as competitors. Then, when you want to end your relationship with a client, you can refer them to these other firms, saying they "can better service your needs." If these relationships really take off, when the smaller firms find themselves too small to handle larger clients, ideally they will refer those clients to you!

13. **Plug the black hole.** Has anyone in your firm ever experienced any of these scenarios? The common theme is that people's billable time vanishes.

   - When you work 8 hours at a client's office, you put 8 hours on your timesheet. When you work the *entire day* in your office on one or more clients, *at best* you record 6 or 7 charge hours.

   - You were in the office all day for the past three days. You know you did nothing but billable work all three days. You fill out your timesheet for the past three days. You search your memory long and hard, but the most you can identify is 11 billable hours. A big part of the problem is that it is very difficult for most people to remember what they did yesterday, let alone the day before.

   - You spent 40 hours on a job, but you know you can bill for only 30 hours. Rather than broadcast a 25% write-off in front of your fellow partners, you record only 30 hours. If you are a staff person, rather than endure the rage of a partner for going over budget, you record only 30 hours.

When valid, billable time goes unrecorded, whether due to loss of memory or lack of courage, the time falls into an abyss that I term the "black hole." As much as 5% of most firm's potential fees falls into the black hole. For a $5 million firm, this adds up to $250,000.

Here's how to close the black hole:

a. Use daily timesheets. These days, almost all firms *provide* for timesheets to be prepared daily. But many firms allow their people to fill out timesheets several days at a time, which defeats the purpose of daily timesheets. Insist they be submitted every day.

b. Establish a very clear firm policy that all time worked on a job must be recorded on timesheets. You need your WIP run to reflect all time spent on a job for at least two reasons: First, you never know. You may be able to bill some of the excess time, either now or later. But if it never hits WIP, it will definitely never get billed. Second, unless all time is recorded, you will under-quote the job next year, thus perpetuating this vicious cycle of underreporting time.

c. Get the staff involved in drafting bills for partners' approval. Often the staff will bill more aggressively than the partners. They did the work and they want their work to be of value to the firm. They may know better than the partners why the time went over budget. There may be a valid reason for the overage that can be billed to the client. The staff know that value was conveyed, and they want their work billed.

d. Communicate time expectations on each job to the staff. Assume there are two identical jobs given to two different staff of equal ability. Staff person A is told that the budget is 30 hours and staff person B isn't told anything at all. Which person do you think will come closer to the budgeted 30 hours?

Learn to profit from closing the black hole.

14. **Find out what your staff thinks of your firm.** Everyone would agree that a well-trained, highly motivated, productive staff is one of the most critically important ingredients to strong levels of success and firm profitability. To achieve this, firms need to assess how their staff feel about the firm, their jobs and their bosses. Firms should periodically conduct a survey of their staff's attitudes. Armed with the survey results, your firm can address the issues raised and make your firm a better place to work. This should make your staff happier, help you reduce turnover, and ultimately increase profitability.

The staff survey should be anonymous and should be conducted by an outside consultant. Unless the staff is 100% convinced that their responses cannot be attributed to them individually, they will not be open and honest. Only an outsider can provide this anonymity and safety. The staff will trust the outsider only if they submit their surveys directly to the outsider.

The firm should consider two types of surveys:

a. General staff surveys that address areas such as performance feedback, training, promotion opportunities, opinions of firm management, adequacy of firm communications, fairness of employee policies, compensation and benefits, and feelings about which partners are pleasant to work with and which are not.

b. Upward evaluation of the partners and perhaps the managers, by the staff (sometimes referred to as "360-degree evaluations"). The most important factor that affects staff retention in any business is the employee's relationship with their boss. At CPA firms, the bosses are the partners and managers. Firms need to make sure that their bosses are good supervisors who are helping the staff learn and grow.

Can you afford *not* to find out what your personnel think about you?

Actually, there is one very good reason *not* to survey your staff. If you have no intention of communicating the results of the survey to the staff or acting on the issues raised, your firm will be better off not doing the survey at all. When a firm conducts such a survey but then does nothing with the findings, this angers the staff. They went out on a limb to give their honest feedback, and then the firm ignored their thoughts. This does more harm than good.

15. **Think of partners as account managers**. The process of deciding which staff to invite into the partnership is an endeavor fraught with danger. We want our new partners to be good at everything: technically strong, good at business development, personable, capable of managing client relationships, credible with the staff, good at training, ambitious, hard-working, loyal. You get the picture. Perfect!

A common reason—though not the *best* reason—staff members get promoted to partner is to keep them. They usually fall short in a few key categories (typically bringing in business and leadership qualities) but we want to reward their loyalty and hard work. The clients like them, they do good work and the partners trust them. But above all else, we don't want to lose them. So we make them partners. At some point, the partners have to be more selective about who they invite to be partners.

One of my clients unofficially calls their firm's partners "account managers." This is a marvelous term to describe what partners *should be*. An account manager delegates as much billable work as possible and focuses on business development, managing client relationships and developing staff. Billable hours for account manager-partners hover around 1,000 per year. Firms like this enjoy high levels of profits.

The CPA business presents its owners with a great opportunity to leverage themselves, something not nearly as available to other professionals such as attorneys, physicians, and many consultants. Partners should function as account managers and not doers. They need to leverage themselves by delegating work to others, who in turn generate profits for the firm. This increases profitability.

16. **Bigger is better.** The research we do each year in the annual *Rosenberg MAP Survey* has consistently shown, generally speaking, that the larger a firm's annual revenue, the higher its profitability. This does not mean that increasing annual fee volume *guarantees* higher profits because the firm still needs to be managed well. But statistically, there is a strong correlation between size and profitability.

Here are the reasons why bigger firms often more profitable:

- They attract larger clients.

- They have an edge on recruiting (though it's never easy).

- They achieve the critical mass to afford full-time professionals in administration, marketing, human resources and technology.

- They use more sophisticated marketing tactics.

- They develop the bandwidth to provide clients with an increasingly diverse portfolio of services, especially in consulting areas. This enables them to better satisfy clients' increasingly sophisticated needs.

- Because bigger firms have more management resources, they usually do a better job at (a) developing and mentoring staff and (b) developing a strong technology infrastructure.

17. **Provide wealth management services.** In the late 1990s, CPA firms began offering wealth management services to clients. But years ago the percentage of firms under $20M providing these services plateaued at only 20-33%. An examination of wealth management services shows they are much more profitable than traditional

CPA firm services. So this is a great opportunity for CPA firms to increase their profitability—and better satisfy their clients' needs.

18. **Decrease 1040 fee volume.** Our research consistently shows that the most profitable firms are those that rely the *least* on 1040s, especially standalone 1040s, for their overall fee volume.

19. **Be busy year-round instead of relying heavily on the tax season to generate the majority of your revenue.** The average CPA firm generates roughly 45-50% of its annual fee volume in the tax season. This skewing effect is often termed "tax season compression." Firms that have a high degree of tax season compression aren't able to efficiently utilize their staff during the remainder of the year. They need to staff up to meet the demands of the tax season, but then scramble to keep the staff busy during the rest of the year. This drags profits down because their staff post disturbingly low annual billable hours. Conversely, firms that can stay busy throughout the year are able to utilize their staff more efficiently, which translates directly to increased profits.

It's important to note that there are two ways to stay busy throughout the year. The first way is to move tax season work outside of the tax season. The second way is to attract different types of work, mainly consulting, that enable the firm to stay busy year-round. Although both approaches will yield positive results, the second approach is usually more effective than the first.

20. **Obtain as much audit work as possible**. Our research shows that firms with a higher percentage of total revenue in the audit area outearn those with small or no audit practices. Audit clients tend to be bigger clients, which is a good thing in and of itself. Additionally, audit clients tend to be the best prospects for cross-selling, which adds further to the firm's profitability.

What Isn't as Important to Profitability as Some People Think

1. **High partner billable hours**. This is very tempting to many partners. They like being busy. They like billable work. It gives them an excuse not to bring in business. They like doing staff-level work because they would rather do the work themselves than train someone to do it and correct their mistakes. But firms with high partner billable hours generally don't do a good job leveraging themselves, ignore their role to train and mentor staff and help them learn and grow, do very little business development and often experience flat growth. My experience is that, at some point, there is an inverse relationship between partner billable hours and income per partner.

   The following adage has been stated several times throughout this book but it bears repeating: *It's more important what partners do with their nonbillable time than their billable time.* Critically important nonbillable activities include developing and mentoring staff, firm management (not administration), business development, teamwork and developing niches and specialties, among many other activities.

   It stands to reason that the higher your billable hours are, the less time you have available for these critical nonbillable activities. And that makes it difficult to be more profitable.

   To be perfectly honest, I must share this anomaly with you. I have seen quite a few firms where the partners are highly billable *and* enjoy outstanding profitability. The only explanation I have for this is that there are exceptions to everything. These firms have some superstar partners, usually coupled with an enviable client list. But firms looking to move their profitability from average to excellent should not try to achieve this shift with higher partner billable hours.

2. **Charging low prices, making the firm more affordable and sparing the partners from the distasteful task of doing business development**. This attitude is a big, big mistake. We discussed in Chapter 3 the four benchmarking metrics that far and away have the highest correlation to profitability. One of those four metrics is strong (not gouging) billing rates.

CPAs are legendary for not enjoying selling. Unfortunately, many misguided firms have a marketing philosophy of being cheap in order to attract new clients. That won't lead to strong profits.

3. **Trying to increase profits by cost cutting.** The CPA firm income statement is very simple compared to many other businesses:

Revenue	XXX
Expenses:	
- Staff salaries	XXX
- Overheads	XXX
Total expenses	XXX
Partner profit	XXX

If you do a careful examination, you will find that most of CPA firms' expenses, even a big part of labor, are fixed. Couple this with the fact that CPA firms are, for the most part, not big spenders. All of this means that there is very little opportunity for CPA firms to increase profits by cutting costs.

Here's what *does* matter: Increase the top line, revenues. How?

- Bring in more business.

- Increase revenue with existing clients.

- Raise billing rates and fees.

- Achieve higher realization through better monitoring of jobs, better training, higher productivity, aggressive quoting, tougher client acceptance standards and other tactics.

There's a saying we have: Increases to the top line drop directly to the bottom line. Well, not totally. But you get the picture.

4. **Following old-school business development tactics.** In the great movie *Field of Dreams,* a farmer in rural Iowa has a consuming dream to convert part of his cornfields to a small baseball park as away to generate revenue for his failing farm. The famous line is "If you build it, they will come." Well, it's Hollywood, so of course the people came.

I'm here to tell you that it doesn't work for CPA firms. One of the oldest philosophies for establishing and growing a CPA firm was a three-pronged strategy: (1) hang out your shingle, (2) sit back and wait for clients, bankers and others to refer business to you and (3) do great work. This strategy may have enjoyed some limited success before the age of CPA firm marketing began in the late 1970s, but it would be a mistake for any firm to completely give up on developing business today.

Proactive business development efforts are required.

5. **Striving for realization at or near 100%.** This was thoroughly addressed earlier in this chapter. When realization rates approach 100%, this signals that billing rates are too low. As we have stated throughout this book, high billing rates have a strong correlation to profitability.

   I coined this phrase many years ago: "You can't take realization *percentage* to the bank, but you *can* take realized *dollars* to the bank." This means that although raising your billing rates may cause your realization *percentage* to sink, you are still better off (more profitable) because your realized revenue *dollars* will increase.

   Firms should aim for a realization percentage of 85-92%.

6. **Using a formula to allocate partner income.** Misguided firms reason that compensation *formulas* will increase profitability because they motivate partners to do the basic things that make the most money for us: Bring in business, manage a large client base and do lots of billable work.

   The folly in this is that formulas reward partner production to the exclusion of other critically important *intangible* factors, such as firm management, developing and mentoring staff, building niches and specialties and teamwork. You get what you reward. If there are no factors for compensating for intangible factors, then they won't get done, or at least won't get done *well*.

   Another drawback to compensation formulas is that partners game the system by hoarding clients and billable hours that should be staff's, thus increasing their income.

7. **Letting the managing partner have the largest or one of the largest client bases to manage.** It's common, though not a best practice, for a rainmaker to be the managing partner. The leadership, interpersonal skills and strength of personality required to be a good business-getter often result in that person commanding the most respect among the partners and thus wielding the most influence. The other partners reason that they are OK with the rainmaker being the MP as long as it doesn't interfere with his or her continuing to bring in lots of business.

   This is counterproductive to the firm because an MP saddled with a large client base can't possibly have enough time to manage the firm properly. And as we have said throughout this book, one of the biggest factors in firm profitability is the quality of management.

8. **Dividing up the administrative duties instead of hiring a firm administrator.** We discussed this earlier. Firms need to have their partners function at a partner level 24/7, and not be bogged down with administrative duties that someone earning a fraction of their compensation can do.

9. **Too much focus on the metric known as "utilization percentage."** This is the number of firm-wide billable hours divided by its total work hours. It is typically measured both for individuals and for the firm as a whole.

   I would like to see firms focus on developing *billable hour targets* for all personnel, including partners, instead of focusing on a percentage. If the target for staff billable hours is 1,700, and they hit it, you shouldn't care much about what the utilization percentage is. Once again, percentages don't generate profits, but billable hours do.

12

50 Great Ways to Improve Profitability

Here's a quick summary of the top 50 profitability tactics discussed throughout this book.

Every successful firm is destined to achieve profitability along a slightly different route. Not all of the practices in this book will be universally applicable. But certain principles, like bringing in clients effectively and developing a great staff, pertain to firms across the board. Few firms excel in all categories, but it can be done. How you get there is up to you and your partners.

There are more than 50 practices and tactics throughout this book for improving you firm's profitability. We have limited this list to the top 50. To some extent, the 50 practices are ranked in order of their impact on firm profitability. But sometimes a tactic's ease of implementation or popularity bumps it higher.

1. **Provide strong management and leadership.** Managing partners' #1 client must be the firm. They shouldn't carry such a large client base that it prevents them from properly managing the firm.

    Firms need an effective management structure. This usually includes not just the managing partner but an executive committee or board and professional, high-level administrative people.

Strong management and leadership are the most important keys to profitability because they make all of the other 49 tactics happen.

2. **As the partners go, so goes the firm**. A major factor in the success and profitability of the firm is the performance of its partners. The firm's management and its partners must have a steely focus on this. It's more important what partners do with their *nonbillable* time than their *billable* time. Partners focus 24/7 on the two main jobs of a partner: taking great care of their clients and taking great care of their staff. Partners should never be too busy with clients to perform critically important duties and tasks.

3. **Maintain high billing rates**; Be a higher-priced, lower-volume firm, not a low price-higher volume operation. If realization gets much above 90%, the firm's rates and fees are probably too low.

4. **Improve leverage** with a high ratio of professional staff to partners.

5. **Increase staff billable hours** by creating production targets and formalizing staff scheduling. Partners never lose sight of one of their main duties: keeping staff busy and productive.

6. **Limit partners' billable hours**. There is an inverse relationship between high partner charge hours and firm profitability. Partners should focus on client relationships and staff development while avoiding doing staff-level work.

7. **Create a strong firm culture** where all personnel, especially the partners, are engaged and committed to the firm's vision, values, strategies and practices. Transgressions are never tolerated because the firm considers them sins.

8. **Adopt and commit to a philosophy that staff are just as important as clients. Make your firm a great place to work,** where staff continuously learn and grow. Staff development and mentoring are important factors in allocating partner income.

9. **Survey your staff to find out what they think** of the firm and then address the issues they raise to improve the firm's practices for managing all areas of staff management.

10. **Conduct periodic upward evaluations of partners and managers by the staff.** To walk the talk on treating staff as well as clients

and to be tenacious in the development of great staff, the firm needs honest feedback on how the staff are being treated, by person.

11. **Provide world-class training** in technical, leadership development, computer and soft skill areas.

12. **Make sure the partners are great bosses**. Establish a culture where partners are a positive, mentoring influence on the staff.

13. **Implement proactive programs to retain a diverse staff** and help them advance in the firm.

14. **Recruit and hire robustly.** Hire the right people the first time. Don't hire just anyone walking through the door with a pulse.

15. **Teamwork rules**. The firm performs at its best when its partners work as a team instead of a group of sole practitioners who happen to sharing staff and overhead.

16. **Adopt the account manager philosophy** of what a partner is. Partners are delegators and relationship people, not doers.

17. **Hire professional administrators, especially a COO or firm administrator.** Keep partners away from administration so they can focus on clients and staff.

18. **Focus on increasing revenues** rather than cutting costs.

19. **Pursue business development proactively**, especially by the partners. When firms stop growing, they stagnate.

20. In addition to seeking rainmakers, get other partners to **generate a little mist.**

21. **Consider a merger.** They're a great way to increase profitability by increasing revenue while acquiring staff and specialty services. But make sure you do mergers right.

22. **Add wealth management** to your services. It has the potential to be more profitable than traditional CPA firm services.

23. **Develop a diverse portfolio of services, especially consulting,** to better satisfy clients' needs and capitalize on the cross-selling poten-

tial. Providing consulting services gives the firm a head start in adjusting to the time when revenue potential for compliance services declines due to technology advances. An added benefit: it keeps your firm busy year-round.

24. **Explore niche marketing and specialization.** Business development is easier when a firm or a partner is perceived as an expert in a specific area. Clients are also willing to pay more for an expert than a generalist.

25. **Bigger is better**. Commit to continuous increasing revenues by organic growth and mergers. Though bigger is not *guaranteed* to be better, in the vast majority of cases, profitability grows in sync with higher revenue.

26. **Perform client satisfaction and loyalty surveys** because they improve client retention, identify client needs and exploit cross-selling opportunities.

27. **Focus business development efforts** on pleasing and expanding relationships with *existing* clients as much as getting *new* clients.

28. **Provide world-class service,** including delivering technically flawless work. To retain clients, expand services to them, receive unsolicited referrals and get them to pay your bills on time without pushback, firms must first super-please those clients.

29. **Cultivate effective partner relationships and communications.** Partners should be on the same page. When partners have good relationships with each other and communicate well, their performance increases. The converse is true at firms with weak partner relations. As the partners go, so goes the firm.

30. **Insist on partner accountability**. If there are no consequences when a partner fails to meet expectations or achieve a goal, then those expectations and goals are less likely to be met.

31. **Base partner compensation on performance.** Incentivize and reward partners to do what the firm *needs* them to do, *every year,* remembering that you get what you reward. No coasting allowed.

32. **Make sure the partners practice effective time management.** Help them understand their priorities and do first things first.

33. **Increase realization** through better job supervision, scheduling, training, fee quoting and change orders, among other tactics.

34. **Create a system for management to review and approve billing write-offs** over a certain dollar value.

35. **Terminate low-profit and otherwise undesirable clients** so you can focus more on A clients. Limit your 1040 work to high-end returns and tax forms connected to businesses. Keep low-priced, standalone returns to a minimum.

36. **Make time for strategic thinking and planning**. Focus more on strategic planning *implementation* (the hard part) than *brainstorming* (the easy part).

37. **Innovate.** Once a reasonable amount of success and profitability is achieved, there is a strong tendency for firms to keep doing things the way they've always done them. Heed this advice from Roberto Goizueta, former Coca-Cola chairman: "If you think you will be successful running your business in the next 10 years the way you did the last 10 years, you're out of your mind. To succeed, we have to disturb the present."

38. **Firms need to get the right people *on* the bus and get the wrong people *off* the bus.** Negative conduct is contagious. If unchecked, it becomes a cancer that quickly infects others, making it difficult to maintain a positive culture where people are engaged and pull in the same direction.

39. **Close the black hole in time recording.** Require partners and staff to turn in timesheets every day.

40. **Use technology** to make your practice more efficient and effective.

41. **Staff should draft client invoices** for partner approval. They will be more aggressive in billing because they are closer to the work and want to see their efforts be converted to revenue.

42. **Communicate time and billable hour expectations to the staff** for each engagement and for the year.

43. **Benchmark** your firm to identify areas that need improvement. Don't be satisfied with merely *meeting* national norms; these are just

averages. Benchmarking should be used to make your firm an *above-average* firm.

44. **Teach the staff the business of public accounting.** Help them understand how CPA firms operate and how they make money. Your staff need to see how they fit into the firm.

45. **Have your administrative staff make (soft) collection calls.**

46. **Join roundtable groups** of both managing partners and firm administrators. Learn from other firms.

47. **Bill the time of administrative staff** when they work on clients.

48. **When monitoring productivity, focus on billable hour *amounts*,** not utilization *percentage*.

49. **Franchise your procedures.** Be dependent on *systems*, not *people*, for how work is performed. Staff should perform certain work projects the same way, regardless of who the supervisor is.

50. **Use your imagination.** Really successful firms all employ some tactic for profitability that wise consultants are unaware of.

My hope is that you take these 50 best practices, along with the more in-depth looks throughout this book, and implement changes to improve your firm's profitability. Change isn't easy, but your firm's ongoing success depends on your ability to drive the initiatives that keep it thriving and financially secure.

Made in the USA
Columbia, SC
16 August 2024

40085965R00076